I0817337

DOUBLE ACTION

Classic Revolvers for Target Shooting, Hunting, and Security

ULRICH SCHWAB

DOUBLE ACTION

CLASSIC REVOLVERS FOR TARGET SHOOTING, HUNTING AND SECURITY

4880 Lower Valley Road • Atglen, PA 19310

Originally published as *Double Action – Revolver-Klassiker für Sport, Jagd und Security* by Motorbuch Verlag, Postfach - Stuttgart, 2011.

Editing by
Ingeborg Schwab

Interior book design by
Jennifer Prosser, TEBITRON GmbH, Gdynia.

Acknowledgments
Konrad Krappmann
Axel Manthei
Volker Raith
Andreas Mauch

Sources
Dean K. Boorman, *Die Waffen von Colt.*
Dean K. Boorman, *Die Waffen von Smith & Wesson.*
Dr. Bruno Brukner, *Faustfeuerwaffen.*
Rainer Emde, *Pistolen und Revolver in Stainless.*
BDS-Sporthandbuch.
DSB-Sporthandbuch.
Caliber, Deutsches Waffen-Journal, Visier.
Frankonia Jahreskataloge.
Wischo-Jahreskataloge.
Various manufacturers and importers.

Translated by Omicron Language Solutions, LLC

Library of Congress Control Number: 2014932258

Designed by Justin Watkinson

ISBN: 978-0-7643-4630-9
Printed in China

Published by Schiffer Publishing, Ltd.
4880 Lower Valley Road
Atglen, PA 19310
Phone: (610) 593-1777; Fax: (610) 593-2002
E-mail: Info@schifferbooks.com

Contents

Introduction

The revolver's future is not as a general-purpose weapon – with a few exceptions. For bodyguards and security services personnel, their compact design, which keeps a weapon both inconspicuous and handy, counts more than firepower or the quickest-possible way to reload. Or for hunters, who can get five or seven shots in a caliber powerful enough for them, even with just a feather-light titanium "snub nose."

Things look very different for target shooters. Here, all the various associations sponsoring revolver shooting offer such broad and varied range of opportunities to practice shooting that just about any possible inclination can be met, both in the design of the weapons as well as the target shooting procedures themselves. With shooting styles ranging from Western to the IPSC [International Practical Shooting Confederation] – of course, always legal and according to the rules – just about anything goes: shooting in single or double action; standing, kneeling, sitting, lying down; one-handed, two-handed, with stipulated "strong" or "weak" shooting hand; from varying distances; and in the free or open classes, with additional weight, muzzle brake, telescopic sight, or red dot reflex sight.

Notwithstanding the fascination that a single-action, hammer-cocked revolver, modeled after the Colt 1873 Single Action Army can exert on the members of some exclusive group of shooters, in general, double action revolvers are, essentially, the standard equipment for target shooting. Smith & Wesson alone, for decades the international trend-setter in this field, offers its double action revolvers in five-, six-, seven-, eight-, and ten-shot models. With a barrel length of 1 7/8 to 8 3/8 inches (48 to 213 millimeters) in the range, and up to 12 inches (305 millimeters) from the performance center. Smith & Wesson also offers revolvers in the calibers .22 l.r. (long rifle), .22 Winchester Magnum Rimfire (WMR), .38 Smith & Wesson Special/ Special + P, .357 Smith & Wesson Magnum, 10 mm auto/.40 Smith & Wesson, .41 Remington Magnum, .44 Smith & Wesson Special, .44 Remington Magnum, .45 Automatic Colt Pistol (ACP), .460 Smith & Wesson Magnum, and .500 Smith & Wesson Magnum. In addition, there are interchangeable systems and additional special features from other manufacturers.

Depending on the application, double-action revolvers differ in the design and installation of the lock action or trigger mechanism. When target shooting is the primary use, shooters almost always use revolvers that are cocked by the hammer and trigger, better known as traditional double-action revolvers, the versatile representatives of using either "simple" or "double movement" for cocking the gun. Firing the gun with single action is recommended for "punching" the ten-spot; double action when the time interval of hits, or time alone, counts. Double-action-only, or DAO-like revolvers, that cannot or only with difficulty be cocked by the hammer, owe their existence to practical experience: a hammer which is either concealed or "shrouded" – only a stub sticks out from the frame – won't get caught in your clothes when you draw the revolver. Finally, as for hunting, single and double action revolvers, or Double Action Only play only a minor role – our fellow huntsmen, climbing up to or down from their raised blinds, are already dealing with their three-barreled guns and mouths, and more likely concerned with the scope and weight of their equipment.

Further criteria for the weapon's specific use are barrel length, in respect to target shooting rules; resistance of non-natural backstops, on which the approved ammunition depends; and the conventional caliber for service and hunting. As a result, in the following work, barrel lengths discussed end at 6 1/2 inches and cartridge strength at .44 Magnum. In this context, revolvers with longer barrels, or in calibers up to .500 Magnum, are only of statistical interest.

Editing, photography, and the manufacturers' and importers' willingness to be accommodating in providing the weapons all presented challenges. But the precision shooting, combined with measuring velocity to determine the bullet energy and the TriggerScan measurements, took even more effort. Once again, Konrad Krappmann provided his assistance, as "Lord of the Rings" and trusted advisor, as he had for the previous works, *Praktisches Pistolenschießen* [*Practical Pistol Shooting*] and *Kleinkaliber-Sportpistolen und Revolver* [*Small Caliber Target Pistols and Revolvers*]. He is a master gunsmith based in Kirchberg an der Murr, with a manufacturing license for hunting and sporting weapons. The results presented at the end of the book for "machine" shooting at 25 meters, do not, in principle, indicate the expected dependence of the gun's shooting performance on its price range. What is really striking, however, is the big difference in the individual models' ammunition compatibility, when there was exclusive use of commercially available factory ammunition.

Axel Manthie, of Kaufering, created the graphic representations of trigger-pull weight and trigger mechanism characteristics based on his unerring measurement techniques. Manthie, a weapons technology engineer and importer of high-quality measurement systems, used the TriggerScan system, which follows the trigger of the cocked weapon by means of a motor-driven measurement arm up to impact and produces a curve to illustrate the resulting pull weight through the applied force with an accuracy of 0.004 Newton (0.408 grams) in recording the force, and 0.025 millimeters in recording the travel. By this method, what is usually only a feeling that can be described subjectively can be made visible on a diagram. In single action, the curve rises steeply over the first stage trigger travel to the firing of the shot, then falls back on the trigger stop or frame impact at the end of trigger travel, and finally runs almost straight back up. The double-action profile shows the pull weight while the cylinder is rotating; when the cylinder stop engages, as the fixed, spring loaded, or rolling catch transfers to hammer and trigger, and release of the hammer, up to a similarly steep rise after impact. There is also general friction and additional resistance that results from deficiencies in workmanship. A good trigger mechanism has a "smooth" curve.

Colt

More Action by Double Action

In 1876, Colt made a significant contribution to ensuring consistent and reliable synchronization of all the trigger mechanism's movable parts, including the pawl (which rotates the cylinder, also called known as a "carrier") and the cylinder stop, by producing a prototype based on the Single Action Army; this prototype, however, did not yet include a swing-out cylinder. Fifteen years after the death of Samuel Colt (1814-1862), William Mason, who continued to run the company, combined the meanwhile-expired Colt patents from 1835 (U.K. and France), 1836 and 1839 (both U.S.A.), for the Peacemaker, with an original design already equipped for shooting metal cartridges with center-fire ignition and with a hand, linked to the hammer, to operate the cylinder, with an appropriately modified, and later repeatedly reworked, trigger mechanism. Based on the Trantner system, patented in 1865, the trigger cocked the hammer by a linked pawl so it engaged in a slot, and took it to freefall over the highest point. An additional notch to allow selective shooting in single action and the safety catch were already standard features, while, in the pre-emptive Colt tradition, the two-step cylinder hand, also linked to the trigger, revolved the cylinder with the first step and, with the second, stopped it until the block clicked into place. With the double-action trigger, the Lightning, manufactured from 1877 to 1910, was also made with a round butt instead of the classic square butt grip.

In today's terms, we'd call the Lightning a big hit. Despite initial difficulties with the mechanism, over 160,000 copies of this first representative of the new generation Colt were sold. This was all the more surprising, since just one year later, Mason patented and began mass production of the Frontier, with a larger frame and reinforced trigger mechanism parts. This model was a .44 or .45, in contrast to the original .38 caliber Lightning. Next, thunder followed the Lightning almost as quickly: the Thunderer, a smaller-sized Frontier, now shot .41 caliber cartridges. In terms of production, however, the larger models were more than two-thirds behind the popular .38s.

Dream Team: Double Action and Swing-Out Cylinder

Since the veteran models could shoot faster, but could not be reloaded faster, these rather clunky and not always reliable double-action models only began to establish themselves against the Single Action Army – both technically well developed and with an unmatched elegance of line – after the introduction of the swing-out cylinder. Another prototype provided the decisive impulse, with a solid frame, by this time an indispensable Colt feature, which made it possible for the now freely accessible cylinder to be swung out sideways, as well as with the related patents of 1881 and 1884. The series was launched in 1889 with the Navy model; in 1892 came the New Army & Navy, and finally the New Series in 1898, of which some 356,000 pieces were produced until 1944. Other models, such as the Official Police, a modified New Army & Navy, sold as many as 425,000 pieces in "public service." The first alternative to the early Colt swing-out cylinder revolvers, made by Smith & Wesson, allowed faster loading and (automatic) case ejection even as break-action guns.

In further development of the double-action trigger, in 1908, Colt, making a newly conceptualized trigger mechanism, replaced the cocking lever linked to the trigger with a spring-loaded catch on the hammer, and thus created the basis for an especially "smooth" trigger mechanism action. This idea actually came from the Belgian manufacturers Mangeot and Comblain, who already in 1853 had adapted a revolver's hammer for pinfire cartridges, using a cutting-edge "flap" or lifter: when the trigger, with its beak-shaped back, was operated, it caught hold under the lifter, up to the "firing" release of the hammer, and to reset, slid along the deflected catch until clicking back into place. Even after Colt simplified the trigger mechanism even further for the Mark III models and the Anaconda, the 1908 version remained in use up to the short-term great white hope Python Elite at the end-phase of its revolver production.

Towards the end of a long series of well-known models of this type, such as the Official Police, Army Special Model 1908, New Service Model 1909, New Service Target Model, Police Special, the famous two-inch Detective Special of 1927, or the Cobra, in 1955, Colt presented what is even today a "sport-type", large-caliber, general use, and target-shooting revolver. A well-maintained and skillfully shot

Python caliber .357 Magnum/.38 Special can still stir up notice at any shooting gallery, at least among the seniors. As one recalls: "Earlier on, wherever someone pulled out a Python, that was it for the entire evening of shooting."

Hale and hearty senior: Colt's Python is a revolver classic. Even over a decade after production stopped, it's still something to contend with on the shooting range. Its qualities in precision and trigger action compete successfully with the stylistic, and discreetly conceals its 1955 vintage with the 1908 trigger mechanism.

Non-Toxic, but not Harmless: Python

A giant among snakes (python reticulatus, reticulate python, Southeast Asia, ten meters; python sebae, rock python, Africa, seven meters); as a revolver, it's masculine. And in today's parlance, a cult object: Colt's steely interpretation of this reptile still shows, except for the newer trigger mechanism, all the essential design features of the first swing-out cylinder revolver, and at the same time represents the highest technical achievement of an entire series. After decades of

Exemplary: The balanced design and such outstanding details as the complex barrel unit, with full, continuous underlug and ventilated barrel rib, have long been general state-of-the art. Only the muzzle profile is still typically Colt.

success, however, even this model has also suffered a significant drop in quality, due to the heavy economic pressure resulting from the many sophisticated guns already on the market, labor disputes, and dwindling government contracts – Colt's Patent Fire Arms Manufacturing Co. in Hartford, Connecticut, was finally so close to ruin that already by the 1980s, this one-time flagship company had to change its name to Colt's Manufacturing Company, Inc. and adopt an austerity budget under new management.

For the Python and other models such as the Detective Special or King Cobra, initially, this meant business as usual; for the Python itself, the full program: blued, rust-resistant and the Ultimate Stainless (rust-resistant and mirror polished), and made in 2 1/2, 4, 6 and 8 inches. At the same time, because image-building was the order of the day, the proprietary Custom Gun Shop was still manufacturing in parallel, for a time, the still impeccably made Python, without taking recourse to modern low-cost production methods. The promising addition of "Elite," as it were, indicated the makers were using every resource. For this elaborate milling, turning and fitting work, however, the customer paid more than twice what he would for comparable competitive models. The German importer Frankonia offered the blued or stainless steel four and six inch models from 1997 to 2004 at prices of up to 1,639 euros. The standard versions, which ultimately cost 1,498 euros (4, 6 and 8 inch, blued), or up to 1,698 euro (4, 6 and 8 inch, polished rust-resistant steel, were omitted from the catalogue by 1998, when production ended.

The Python, also as a typical representative of the original Colt concept – with the cylinder closed frame; the trigger action mounted on the left in the frame; the trigger controlled right rotation of the cylinder; with the cylinder crane swinging out left; cylinder lock in the ejector star; cylinder stop in the hammer end position; case ejection through the cylinder pin – differs substantially in almost all components from its direct or indirect predecessors. The .357 Magnum caliber alone required a much more stable design. In comparison to the K or L frame models from Smith & Wesson discussed below, for example, the .357 appears more like a .44 – frame length, frame walls and the trigger-backstrap distance, without counting the grip panels, are close to those of an M 29/629. Only at the front end and on the crane, does the N frame feature a correspondingly more substantial barrel thread diameter and cartridge capacity. The weapons' unloaded weights differ only minimally, due to different barrels and cylinders. Shooting a double-action Python, therefore, would be more something for a strong "long-finger."

Blued or in stainless steel, the latter increasingly in demand because of current taste, the Python's basic parts are manufactured from forged blanks or forged from solid block material – which allegedly, by the way, was done with dwindling precision, and ever more under fire, due to progressive automation in the early-1970s.

The section around the long barrel thread and swung-out crane, the bridge and the breech face to the firing pin and locking bolt bores especially show the solid character of the frame. In the transition to the grip and below, two windows open for the square butt. The angular grip frame was kept short so that it can take the lower drawn combat grip, in addition to the traditionally shaped grip.

Cylinder and crane are screwed as a unit in the cylinder pivot by the spring-loaded ejector rod and ejector star hub, and connected by the crane's bearing pin with the frame. The pin rotates somewhat more than 90 degrees in a longitudinal bore under the cylinder, and is secured with a ring groove and a spring-loaded pin on the frame right side, from damage when the cylinder swings out. The crane pivot angle and backward shift of the cylinder limit impact on the frame and lock plate.

The fluted cylinder holds six cartridges; the locking grooves, like the cylinder stop, are slightly offset in the frame in relation to the chambers. This structure does not weaken critical points as much as milled cutouts directly over the bores. Rotation-direction chamfers guide the sliding pawl into position. The trigger-controlled cylinder movement pawl and ejector star ratchet rotate the cylinder.

Force is transmitted by profiling of the ejector star hub, which is moved lengthwise by the ejector rod, the congruously profiled guide bushing in the cylinder, and two pins in the cylinder base. A second guide bushing in the crane hollow shaft also forms the mainspring retainer.

For Colt, the cylinder lock has always been a one-sided affair. The same is true for the Python cylinder, which is only locked with the 6.4 millimeter-thick locking bolt in the frame; this catches 1.5 millimeters deep into the center of ejector star, and its 31 millimeter hub ensures a strong enough hold. However, the cylinder assembly clearance on the crane hollow shaft and the crane bearing together create a misalignment, something inconceivable with the best kind of double lock. To unlock, the slide-shaped left cylinder plate pulls the locking bolt on the coupling hub from the cylinder star. The slider runs counter to a spring in the lock plate.

The 1908 trigger mechanism, basically unaltered, is mounted beneath the doubly screwed cover. In the Python – instead of separate trigger and main springs, such as were used starting from 1969 in meanwhile long since retired models such as the Official Police Mark III, Trooper Mark III, or Lawman Mark III – a two-sided V-shaped main spring has everything, as it were, under control. There are two smaller helper springs, only to keep the hammer lifter and cylinder stop in place.

All-rounder: This One Can Do Anything

The mainspring in this complex system does a lot, as demonstrated not only by the force distribution between trigger and hammer, but also by what has been known since 1905 as the Colt Positive Lock automatic shock and drop safety. The upper side of the spring's V powers the hammer directly, in a sense, via a chain link, while the lower side, supported on a long lever mounted in the backstrap, exerts indirect pressure on all the other parts. The tip of this lever engages in the left

In the Python, instead of separate springs for trigger and hammer, the traditional V-shaped spring served all the parts. With the trigger mechanism un-cocked, the spring is spread wide between the hammer stirrup and the reset lever, which controls the hammer reset, the cylinder stop, the cylinder hand, and the hammer block.

side of the trigger-linked cylinder hand, or cylinder hand, springs it into position in the ejector star ratchets, makes frictional connection with the trigger by the pawl bearing and its right-linked safety catch, controls the hammer return, after which it is named, and also guides the self-sprung cylinder stop in the form of another lever under the safety catch – a true all-rounder. The safety catch rotates around the hammer pin, and raises or lowers the L-shaped safety, mounted at right in the frame; this will only release the firing pin when the hammer is cocked to fire a shot. Then the hammer springs back, through profiles on its underside

When the trigger mechanism is cocked, the two spring legs are barely apart. The upper puts pressure on the engaged hammer, the lower on the pawl-latched reset spring.

which slide over each other and the reset lever, until the safety re-engages at the required distance from the frame.

Trigger and hammer are mounted on two fixed pins in the frame and, depending on whether the gun is fired in single or double action, are meshed with each other by two fixed and one movable catch. There is a long tip or "beak" on the trigger; when the hammer is cocked, this is lifted by the hammer until it clicks into place in the cock notch, or when the trigger is pulled, acts as a pawl or catch until the hammer drops. The hammer guides the second fixed catch (the

Milled cutouts in the right frame wall hold the impact and drop safety for the un-cocked hammer, known since 1905 as the Colt Positive Lock. The safety catch linked to the trigger turns around the hammer pin and force guides the L-shaped safety into secured or unsecured position. The cylinder stop lever is under the safety catch.

sear), both through the "beveled" cock notch and the movable catch, the spring-loaded hammer lifter, to cock the trigger. Then come the safety stop under the striking surface, the radius for the reset lever which turns on it, and the track to the upper leg of the mainspring V.

The once-vaunted trigger mechanism is still highly praised today, due to the geometry of the limited bearing clearances, the honed anti-friction surfaces, and its well-coordinated action sequence. In this area, the Python, including pieces manufactured during lower-quality production years, competes successfully with revolvers equipped with trigger mechanisms which utilize the reduced friction by an intermediary roller when shooting in double action. Only the release of the cylinder stop lever on the reset lever can still be perceived both acoustically and visually (in the TriggerScan profile).

In single action, the hammer moves the trigger from the reset position against the pressure of the spring-loaded reset lever, backwards until it catches in the cock notch.

One-sided cylinder lock by a strong bolt at the center of the ejector star. For unlocking, the latch-shaped left cylinder plate is responsible.

The trigger simultaneously releases the cylinder stop by the reset lever, pulls the hammer safety from the hammer travel path, and rotates the cylinder by the cylinder hand and ejector star ratchets to the next chamber. As it rotates, the two-step cylinder hand moves to the next tooth and secures the cylinder against moving backwards until the cylinder stop re-engages. The timing is designed so that the cylinder halts approximately at the same time as the trigger clicks into the notch on the hammer, and within the play of the cylinder stop and cylinder hand, the next chamber is aligned with the barrel. The cocked trigger is now right before impact; it will be stopped immediately after the shot is fired, by the cylinder hand's second "step" on the indentation. After the shot is fired, the released trigger swings by the hammer catch, used only in double action, and back to the starting position. The cylinder hand and the hammer safety lever, moving opposite, are forced to follow the rotation, while the down-pulled reset lever again positions the hammer away from the frame and firing pin.

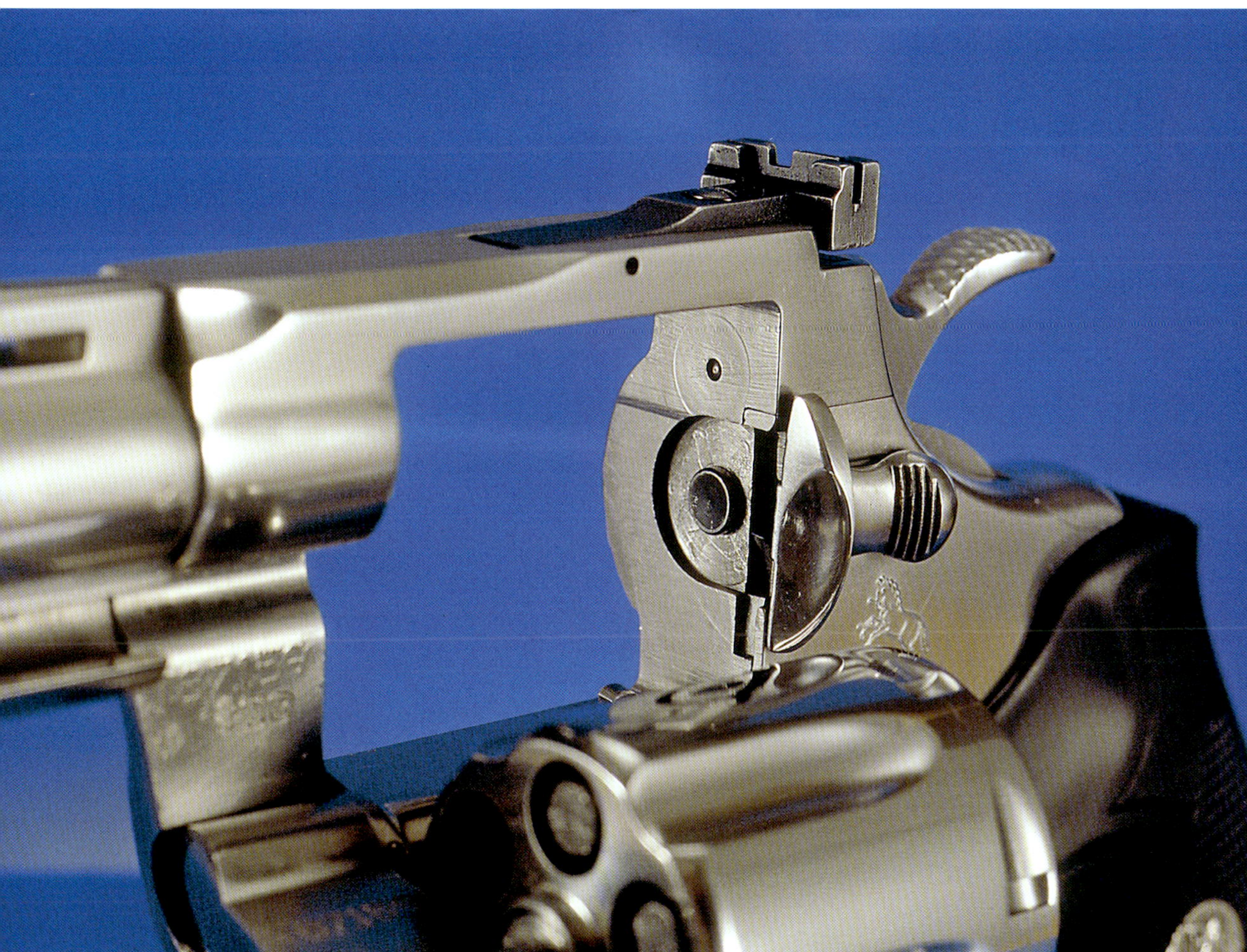

In double action, after short initial travel, the trigger catches on the movable catch and guides the hammer backwards until it drops, without using another catch as Smith & Wesson revolvers do. This shortens the hammer travel by about seven millimeters, in comparison to single action. As in single action, the trigger takes the linked cylinder hand and hammer safety directly with it, and, with the raised reset lever and cylinder stop pulled along with it, releases the cylinder to rotate. However, since all the movements are controlled by the upper side of the trigger "beak' or tip, and the top turns away far above the cock notch, this time the cylinder stop re-engages together with the release of the hammer. The timing thus halts the cylinder when the shot is fired. The rest of the sequence corresponds to single-action mode.

Selective operation of the trigger of the – in view of the target-shooting 1,000-gram rule – slightly "relaxed" T 87159, results in pull weights of 12.0/34.91 Newton or 1.22/3.56 kilopond, using the terminology still in general use among shooters. The TriggerScan profile shows wide amplitude after the directly cocked hammer is released, presumably due to the uncontrolled vibrations of the relaxed mainspring, as well as a very flat and uniform course for the double-action trigger curve. Subject to the restriction of insufficient impact energy, due to the use of special factory ammunition, with this trigger, it is possible to fire a both rapid and precise series of shots in challenging competitions.

The appearance of this once-impressive revolver, still an attractive piece today, is largely characterized by the barrel, the muzzle profile, the ventilated barrel rib with integral front ramp sight, and the long underlug. With all the versions with barrel lengths ranging between 2 ½ and 13 ½ inches (special equipment) in Royal Blue, with nickel or Colt Guard finish, and the option of stainless steel, brushed or polished, (4 to 8 inches), in the end, only the rust-resistant four- and six-inch models were being manufactured. The 152 millimeter barrel has six left-twist grooves in the groove/land diameter of 8.99/8.8 millimeter, a six-millimeter-long forcing cone from 9.4 to 9.05 millimeters, and lightly chamfered muzzle. The reflex-reducing front ramp sight rises smoothly from the frame bridge and, as a counterpart to the elevation and windage adjustable Colt Accro rear sight, includes a double-pinned ramp front sight with orange plastic insert. For target shooters, it is recommended to replace this Quickdraw sight, intended for general use, with a less photosensitive front sight. The long underlug keeps the Python in good balance during firing.

Colts Last Reptile: Anaconda

The Anaconda is also one of the giant constrictors. It is the largest in the New World and can grow up to eight meters long. Colt designed its biggest reptile for the .44 Magnum caliber. However, the Anaconda first "hatched out" in 1990 – thirty-five years after Smith & Wesson introduced this cartridge and its companion M 29. The Anaconda combined the relatively simple technology of the newer Colts from 1969, with the Python silhouette; pricewise, it is oriented to veterans: after all, even as remainders, after production was stopped, the four- and six-inch models of these American giant snakes cost some 1,539 euros at the turn of the millennium.

The quality comparison is just as distinct. While the Python, even in difficult times, could still be certain of getting conscientious care for its sophisticated design, the Anaconda, even in its developmental stage, had to take the consequences of its manufacturer's economic problems. Although Colt's new management held rigidly to the traditional material requirements, as far as this affected the new arrivals' structure, when it came to workmanship and equipment, they made immense sacrifices. As a result, a later piece from the second generation (after 1993) shows just these sacrifices: unevenly machined surfaces; sometimes razor-sharp, sometimes polished rounded edges; deep milling traces in the cylinder window and inside the frame; and unpolished precision-casting remnants in the trigger mechanism. In fit, timing, and shooting performance, the Anaconda is, however, not far behind the Python.

As to frame construction, the Anaconda is a powerfully reinforced King Cobra, as it was produced from 1986, with barrel lengths of 2 ½ to 8 inches, an un-slotted barrel rib, a forward-beveled underlug reaching to the muzzle, and the Colt Accro rear sight, as a less-expensive alternative to the Python. As a result, the drop-forged, stainless-steel frame features the same small trigger guard, in which the finger, according to the general opinion of shooters, gets claustrophobia, and the matching small round butt with plenty of space for the later-manufactured measured grips. Moreover, the dimensions of the CNC machined parts compare to the requirements of the "big" Magnum cartridges. The wall thickness at the crane, barrel thread, and the entire right side up to well into the grip, is up to 5.5 millimeters; the bridge measures 17 x 6.5 millimeters. Beyond this, the cross-dowelled carbide guide bushing of the rebounding firing pin protects the breech face.

Anaconda: Outwardly a .44 Python, with similar cylinder lock.

The crane, the large-volume six shot-cylinder, and its accessories differ from the older design not only due to caliber. The cylinder stop of the Mark Ill trigger mechanism technology, set closer to the middle, its space requirements, and the space for transmitting the impact pulse by the transfer bar system all affect the construction. The crane bearing pin is just 14 millimeters longer and 7.8 millimeters thicker, with an assembly clearance and its affect on the lateral cylinder play, which are not reduced when the hammer is un-cocked. When the hammer is cocked, or in double action, the cylinder hand, aligned exactly on the ratchet, noticeably reduces this play or wiggle. The locking grooves on the right-rotating cylinder are set just behind the chamber vertex, and the locking bolt, which reaches a further 1.5 millimeters into the center of

Beneath the surface, the Mark III series hammer strut action replaces the reset lock. The transfer bar linked to the trigger moves in an L shape around the above-mounted cylinder hand and first moves into firing position when the trigger is pulled. Before that, transmitting the impact impulse is blocked.

the ejector star, measures less than five millimeters. Finally, the ejector spring was no longer screwed into the hollow shaft of the crane.

Instead of the 1905 Colt Positive Lock hammer safety, in the 1969 version, a hammer strut (transfer bar) takes care of impact and drop safety. The system is strongly influenced by the first automatic revolver safety, created by Norwegian-born Iver Johnson in 1892 in Fitchburg, Massachusetts when he constructed his Safety Automatic Model revolver: a rod linked to the trigger, which only makes contact between the hammer and firing pin when the trigger is pulled. Colt simply omitted making this rod, which would also serve as a cocking lever. When the trigger is released, the hammer is secured at a safe distance from the firing pin on the frame.

Inner workings of the Anaconda: cylinder crane, cylinder, ejector rod with spring, star and locking bolt, lock plate, cylinder thumb latch, trigger, cylinder hand, hammer strut, hammer with fixed (sear) and moveable catches (hammer lifter), mainspring and mainspring rod. Trigger spring and cylinder stop are already installed.

Trigger, cylinder stop, hammer, and the attached catches are precision castings of the highest quality, which do not deserve the obvious casting seams and rough ribbing, which make a poor comparison to the quality machined parts. Cast-on guide rings and ring segments minimize the side-play of trigger and hammer on the frame-fixed pivots. Other features of both parts include a nose on the front of the trigger, which – instead of the Python trigger mechanism's reset lever – lifts the (in this case floating) cylinder stop against the pressure of its spring and over an angular face to click in again. The beak or lip on the opposite side comprises the pawl to click the hammer into the notch in single action, the smoothed control cam for the movable hammer catch for double action, a pin to support the trigger spring and hinge the transfer bar, and another pin to attach the cylinder hand. From the underside of the trigger, a small Allen screw regulates the trigger stop on the frame. On the hammer are the thumb safety for the firing pin; the tension arm or sear with cock notch, the laterally inserted catch with spring and pin, and the socket for the ball head of the mainspring rod. The mainspring is a long coil spring, which is supported on a plate at the bottom of the grip frame. A cross bore in the rod makes it easier to remove and replace the spring fastened there.

When the hammer is cocked, the hammer lifts the trigger into the cock notch. In this movement, the trigger nose releases the cylinder stop, which springs back immediately and moves over the cylinder to the next groove. The pawl rotates the cylinder without moving to the next indent; behind the pawl, the transfer bar moves between the hammer and the firing pin. To halt the cylinder, the cylinder stop engages before the pawl exits from the ratchet. After the shot is fired, the released trigger sticks its nose back into the cylinder stop and pulls the linked bar out of its range.

In the combination of cocking and shooting, the simple trigger mechanism develops a remarkable radial run-out. In the hands of an experienced gunsmith, its relatively high pull weight would certainly not be at any fixed magnitude. In double action, the rounded top of trigger guides the hammer the moveable catch over the point of no return, and, if the trigger stop is well centered, barely falls through. Cylinder stop, pawl and transfer bar follow the same automatic motion as in single action, and the timing brings the cylinder to a stop, just before the hammer drops. In the pictured AN 12076 (see p 27), all the chambers are exactly aligned with the barrel.

Anaconda

The Anaconda's appearance is almost the same as the Python's. The large frame and the .44 barrel match well and, despite the larger mass, maintain a flowing line. The revolver's image is again dominated by the stylistically successful three-pack: barrel, ventilated barrel rib, and long underlug; the stepped front ramp sight with its slight rise from the frame bridge to muzzle reinforces the visual impression. The frame area around the barrel threading and crane, the crane itself and the setting of the frame bridge show the typical profile, and behind them, the smooth-faced flanks form the window to accommodate the 44.5 x 44.5 millimeter cylinder. The rounded grip frame is practically hidden under black neoprene with finger grips.

Extended transfer bar between hammer and firing pin.

With cylinder hand and transfer bar out of the way, the trigger's final contact with the hammer lifter is visible in double action.

Technically, the second generation .44 barrel, just 150.65 millimeters long, does not have a chamfered muzzle; instead, the muzzle is recessed by 1.35 millimeters. When drawn (during manufacturing), it expands less; the muzzle protects the "active" barrel end when the revolver is fired. Colt also designed a new profile for the new barrel, with six left-twist grooves in a groove/land ratio of 10.95/10.55 millimeters (based on AN 12076's dimensions), and selected a twist rate of 508 millimeters. Overlap between forcing cone and chamber opening is 11.5 to 10.9 millimeters, and the air gap measures 0.14 millimeters. The Accro rear sight and ramp front sight are Colt standards.

Colt Python and Anaconda/6 inch, Technical Specifications and Prices

Manufacturer	Colt's Manufacturing Company, Inc., Hartford, Connecticut, U.S.A.	
Model	**Python**	**Anaconda**
Caliber	.357 Magnum/.38 Special	.44 Magnum/.44 Special
Version	Stainless steel, milled, polished, brushed. Fluted cylinder	Stainless steel, milled, polished, peened. Fluted cylinder
Weight	1,298 g	1,440 g
Cylinder capacity	6 cartridges	
Length	290 mm	296 mm
Width	39.5 mm	45.5 mm
Height	144 mm	147 mm
Trigger-backstrap distance with combat grip panels	SA 82 mm DA 93 mm	SA 77 mm DA 91 mm
Grip angle	110 degrees	
Grip	Combat	
Barrel	152 mm, six grooves, left twist	150.65 mm, six grooves, left twist
Cylinder diameter	39.5 mm	45.5 mm
Cylinder length	39.6 mm	45.5 mm
Cylinder gap	0.16 mm	0.14 mm
Trigger pull weight *	SA 12.0 N/1.22 kp DA 34.91 N/3.56 kp	SA 17.52 N/1.79 kp DA 47.64 N/4.86 kp
Sight length/sight radius over barrel axis	193 mm/19 mm	197 mm/22 mm
Rear sight width/ Front sight width	3.1 mm/3.25 mm	3.1 mm/3.25 mm
Price incl. VAT (Remainders)	1,698 euros (1998)	1,539 euros (2004)

*TriggerScan measurements

Trigger Pull Profile [N/mm]

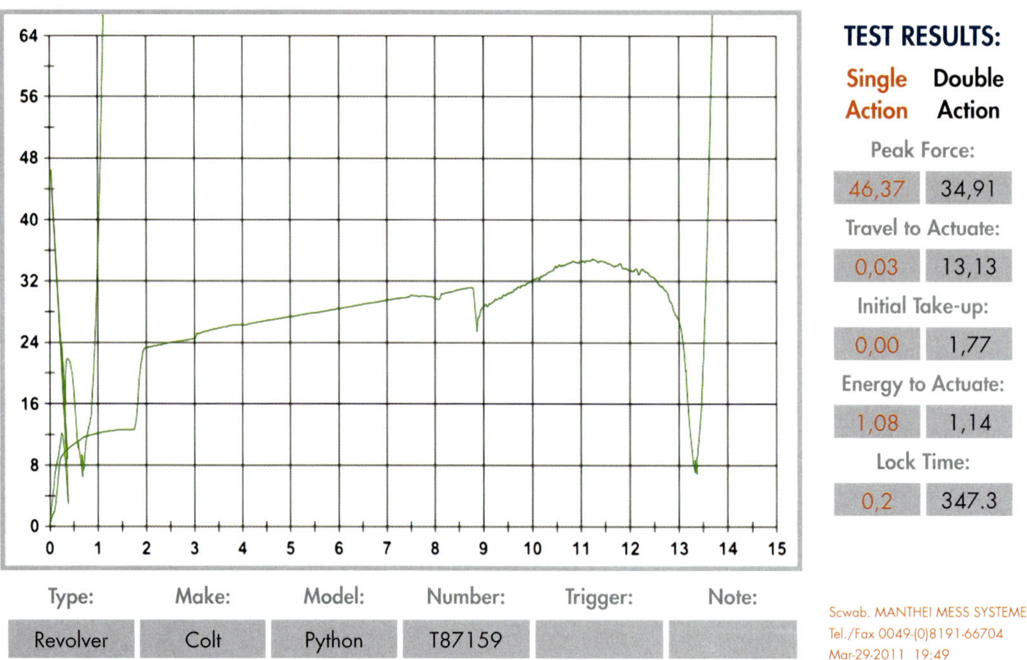

Vibrations after shot release in single action overlie the trigger weight pull of 12.0 Newton.

Trigger Pull Profile [N/mm]

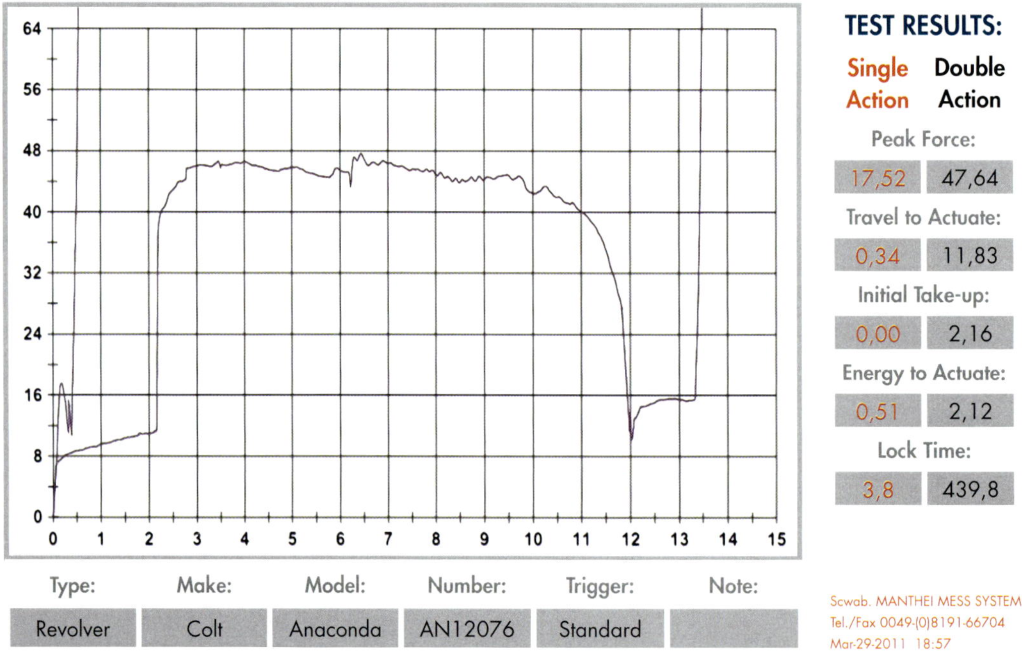

Anaconda

Smith & Wesson

From Top Break to Swing-Out Cylinder

The top break revolver, also known at the high point of its development as a double-action revolver with automatic cartridge case ejection, and with a total distribution of 1.75 million pieces in all calibers ranging from .32 to .45, was at one time an excellent deal for Horace Smith and Daniel Baird Wesson. This revolver, however, rapidly lost its competitiveness against to the first mass-produced swing-out cylinder revolvers from Colt: the Navy Model (1889), New Army & Navy (1892) and New Service (1898). The great American rival profited greatly from the advantages of its solid frame, combined with the sideways swing-out cylinder of its double-action models.

Smith & Wesson, as the company of these long-term business partners has been called since their merger in 1858 into a registered trading company in Springfield, Massachusetts, first responded to the decline in government contracts and further market contractions, after a slow start, in 1896, with the .32 Hand Ejector First Model. This revolver, with a solid frame and swing-out cylinder, now followed the trend, after, however, an initially pessimistic assessment by their makers sent its previously highly esteemed automatic cartridge case ejection into an unearned retirement. In fact, "hand ejection" meant nothing more than operating it by hand rather than automatically. Nevertheless, already by 1898, Smith & Wesson were going one better, with the .38 Hand Ejector in .38 caliber Long Colt, and in 1899 with the .38 Hand Ejector Military & Police, for the new, more powerful cartridges.

SMITH & WESSON

The.38 Special Hand Ejector, brought to maturity in 1902, showed just how good Smith & Wesson's response to Colt's challenge was: this revolver, according to well-known experts, for a long time was the best revolver ever. The six shot, four inch model for the now ultimate .38 Smith & Wesson Special, is a six-time millionaire (!), and still today, with all its alterations and improvements as the Model 10 .38 Military & Police, keeps its unique design and is distributed worldwide.

Long-Time Record Holder: the K Frame

Compared to the first .32 and .38 Hand Ejectors with the "overhead" cylinder stop, the .38 Hand Ejector Military & Police stops the cylinder from below, in a frame reinforced for the cartridges. It was the first representative of the subsequent K series – all of Smith & Wesson's newer revolvers are categorized according to their frame size, as the series M, I, J (small frame), K (medium frame), L (medium frame), N (large frame) and X (extra-large frame). The particularly light I frame, which was developed around 1896 for the lighter caliber revolvers, ended its career in the middle of the last century, in favor of the J frame. The petite M frame was part of the original LadySmith .22 Hand Ejector from 1902 to 1921, and the X frame, as an artillery platform for the .460 caliber and .500 Magnum, at this point is simply subject to the thematic caesura. The K frame's outstanding features include a good fit for the average sized hand, the features of the apparently timeless single- and double-action trigger mechanism, also prized in the bigger frames by shooters and tuners alike, and the overall solid workmanship.

Pointing the way for the series which followed, the steel frame – originally manufactured from forged blanks and from 1993 milled from a solid block in CNC machining centers – forms a solid unit with yoke and bridge around the left swing-out cylinder; it encloses the covered trigger mechanism, including the cylinder hand and the cylinder stop on the opposite side. Since the change over to more rational production processing, the angular grip design, a square butt with applied fine wood grip panels, has been eliminated. Instead of the beloved classic, this frame, like the others, now only features the round butt with rubber or neoprene grip, with wood grip panels added for special models.

On the front, just under the barrel thread, the cylinder crane does its work. This elegant integrated part swings on a bearing pin, which is held by a spring loaded pin in the front lock plate screw, and guides the cylinder on a hollow shaft. The namesake of the hand ejector, the manually operated ejector rod, works in the shaft bore with the ejector star hub screwed to it, and the ejector spring. These have a joint front retainer on the ejector rod, to prevent or reduce pressure on the cylinder, and friction between cylinder and the crane. Positive fit between ejector star and relief-milled cylinder base.

Size comparison: Smith & Wesson has categorized its "biddable" – as the hunters say – or usable general purpose revolver, which are also suitable for target shooting, as J, K, L, and N frame models. Typical representatives are, below, the M 10 .38 Military & Police; above, the M 60 Chief's Special Magnum, M 686 Distinguished Combat Magnum, and M 629 Classic. X frame models for caliber .460 and .500 Smith & Wesson Magnum enjoy a special status.

Cylinder capacity in .357 magnum: five shots in the Chief, six in the M 686, seven in the M 686 Plus, and another six in the unfluted N frame cylinder of the M 627 Target Champion.

Since the start of CNC manufacturing, rod and bearing profiles have replaced the dowel pins and groove of the previous alignment. As the last coaxial member of this complex composite, the independently spring-loaded stay bar (cylinder pin) takes over locking the swiveled-in cylinder in the center of the cylinder plate. Its back end juts out of the ejector star. In front, the ejector rod head rests on a tapered spring bolt, which, depending on the placement of the gun barrel, is open-mounted or set in different length underlugs. To unlock, the cylinder release slide presses the stay bar out of the cylinder plate and against the unlatching spring bolt at the same time.

Without basically changing the trigger action, the weapons' respective level of development and their specific requirements have left their mark on their functional mechanics. The shape, part dimensions, materials, workmanship and alignment of the firing pin (hammer with movable ignition, which strikes through an opening in the breech face on the primer cap, or a rebounding

firing pin mounted in the frame) marked the change of generation, as well as, for example, increasingly easier use for target shooting, or stylistic adaptation for special models. A total of seven essential parts define the trigger mechanism or action: hammer and trigger with pawls, notches and catches for shooting with pre-cocked hammer or double action trigger; the mainspring mounted in the hammer stirrup; the slide with trigger spring, trigger stop, safety cam and hammer block catch; the hammer block; the cylinder hand; and the cylinder stop. Movement of the parts also generates the triple automatic safety mechanism: the return of the dropped hammer (hammer reset), the hammer block which works as additional impact and drop safety, and regulation of the whole system with the thumb safety of the cylinder release when the cylinder is swung open.

Old hand: The six-shot M 10 .38 Military & Police has been in service since 1902. The silhouette alone is still true to the original.

The timing provides information about the quality of the action; this is the timed coordination of the movements in single and double action, including cylinder rotation. Only when positions come together, does the gun really

Comparing the M 10 and M 586 trigger mechanisms shows that, practically, the only differences are in the materials: MIM components in the M 10, color case hardened steel in the M 586. The main components are hammer and trigger, with notches, tip and catches to cock hammer and trigger, the firing pin (M 586) and the striking surface for the firing pin (M 10), the stirrup with mounted flat spring and the trigger-linked strut.

Under the hammer, are the slide with enclosed trigger spring, the trigger stop, the safety pin and the cam to control the hammer reset. In front, are cylinder stop, cylinder hand at right on the trigger, and hammer block on the slide. In an un-cocked M 10 trigger mechanism, slide and block secure the hammer; in the M 586 ready to fire, deactivated safeties free the hammer travel path.

MIM hammer with striking surface for the frame mounted firing pin; steel hammer with movable hammer pin.

work: the perfect interaction of trigger, hammer, safety, cylinder movement, and cylinder stop. Guidance depends on the five catches and three transmission elements: the sear and the movable catch (hammer lifter) of the hammer; the cylinder stop catch; the cock notch latch (tip with notch surface) and the trigger cocking lever; the trigger bar, the slide and the cylinder movement pawl.

In single action, the trigger tip catches hold of the notch on the hammer sear.

Single action, the "simple action" by the hammer, facilitates the trigger mechanism clicking into place at comparatively high cocking and cylinder movement resistance, and reduces the trigger pull weight on the friction of the moving parts, the force of the springs, and the mainspring tension by its strain screw in the frame. The minimum value can be adjusted quite easily, to comply with target shooting regulations. During cocking, the sear engages under the tip, and guides the trigger against the proportional spring force, up to the tip engaging into place backwards. The ready-to-fire hammer and trigger are now right at their backward stroke; to fire a shot, the only thing still required is that well-known, sensitive touch of the fingertip. Still in motion, the pulled trigger presses the spring loaded slide backwards by the linked trigger bar, and, until the shot is released, guides both slide cam and hammer block out of the way of the hammer travel path. The cylinder stop catch on the front of the trigger, moves the floating cylinder stop from the groove above. From the back, the cylinder hand, spring mounted between cocking lever and trigger bar, guides the ejector star ratchet and rotates the cylinder until the cylinder stop clicks into place, one chamber to the left. After the shot is fired, the released trigger swings back into its initial position, again latches into the cylinder stop, pulling the cylinder hand from the ratchet. The slide then again lifts the hammer block into the gap between hammer and frame, and secures the hammer in the reset position.

In double action, "double movement" by the trigger, cocking and cylinder movement resistance comes fully into play in the trigger pull weight. For shooters with smaller hands, this also means that firing a shot demands uncomfortably long trigger travel from the initial position until the hammer drops. An additional potential problem can be posed by the hammer travel, which is shorter by nearly four millimeters. With lower pre-tension of the mainspring, this may not deliver enough impact energy for the hammer cocking function. In short, it is necessary to practice double action shooting, and master it technically. A trigger pull weight under 40 Newton often demands more than just good intentions.

Moving against the hammer movement, the direct-operated trigger catches hold with its top-rounded tip and the cocking lever alternately under the hammer's movable and fixed catches, and cocks it past the cock notch, ready for a free drop. Simultaneously, the trigger disengages the cylinder stop, releases the hammer by the trigger bar, the trigger spring, and the slide from the reset position, pulls the hammer block from the frame with the back-moving slide, and starts the cylinder rotation by the cylinder hand. After a half turn to the next chamber, the cylinder stop springs back up, moves over the cylinder in its characteristic track, and engages, well before the hammer has dropped. A shooter who knows how to fire in double action, will by then have accelerated the rotation and then, with a slight delay, guide the hammer away by the cocking lever. Depending on the gun's design, the next chamber aligns more or less exactly with the barrel, as the cylinder stop engages. If requirements are on a higher scale, the gunsmith or tuner will again have something to do. After the shot is fired, the released trigger renews contact with the cylinder stop. Trigger spring and slide reactivate the hammer safety, and the tip slides along the compressed hammer catch, back to the starting position. A new cycle can begin. To prevent the cylinder accidentally turning past the un-cocked hammer during the "barrage," the released trigger should catch into the cylinder stop and under the movable hammer catch nearly simultaneously. If the tip does not engage in time, it will have no impact on the still-compressed catch.

K Frame Models

For decades, K frame models were made in up to twelve calibers – including older ones, or those less common for revolvers, such as .22 Remington Jet Magnum, .32-20 Winchester, .32 Smith & Wesson, .32 Smith & Wesson Long, .32 Smith & Wesson Long Wad Cutter, 8 mm Lebel, and 9 mm Parabellum – and with a variety of features. Short-barreled general purpose weapons, longer versions with target sights, and small-caliber target shooting weapons, provided an almost complete range for both practical and target shooting requirements. Famous models have come and gone; including such pieces as the "masterpiece" M 14 K-38 (1940) and M 16 K-32 Masterpiece (1946). Or, they remain, such as the M 10 .38 Military & Police (1902) or the M 17 K-22 Masterpiece (1940), the latter as an M 617 in stainless steel. The M 19 .357 Combat Magnum (1955) got a very special role. This wished-for child of the American authorities, combined the size and weight of a .38 with the .357 Magnum caliber, reserved till then only for N frame models, and developed, with an initially moderate ammunition assembly, into one of the most popular service weapons. Any doubts about its durability arose only as cartridge capacity increased; this eventually led to the L frames. Up to 2004, six basic models and several special models were still available in Germany, in calibers .22 l.r., .38 Special and .357 Magnum/.38 Special.

In double action, the trigger tip moves from the initial position (1) to the spring-loaded catch of the hammer …

… (2) and guides it steadily backwards …

3

… (3, 4) until it transfers to the sear.

4

5

(5) As the action continues, the hammer lifter loses contact (6), since the cocking lever stops the trigger until just before the hammer drops …

… (7) Immediately after the shot is fired …
… (8) the safety cams steer the hammer by the forward slider, back into reset position ...

9

… (9, 10), while the trigger tip, as the trigger is being released, moves along the compressed hammer lifter …

10

11

… (11, 12) and finally

12

... (13) Returns to the initial position.

In 1955, Smith & Wesson first entered the .357 class with a K frame model. The M 19 .357 Combat Magnum was the wished-for child of the American authorities; until the introduction of the L frame models in 1981, it found a worthy successor in the M 66 .357 Combat Magnum.

K Frame Models in Germany

Importers	Wischo-Jagd- und Sportwaffen GmbH & Co. KG, Erlangen, Germany Albrecht Kind GmbH (Akah), Gummersbach, Germany					
Model	**Version**	**Caliber**	**Barrel length**	**Cylinder capacity**	**Weight***	**Price (incld. VAT)**
M 617 K-22 Masterpiece	Stainless steel	.22 l.r.	4"/102 mm	10 cartridges	about 1,160 g	€ 859 (2004)
M 617 K-22 Masterpiece	Stainless steel	.22 l.r.	6"/152 mm	6 cartridges 10 cartridges	about 1,280 g about 1,270 g	€ 899 (2010) € 882 (2004)
M 617 K-22 Masterpiece	Stainless steel	.22 l.r.	8 3/8" /213 mm	6 cartridges	about 1,350 g	€ 927 (2004)
M 617 Target Champion	Stainless steel (matte)	.22 l.r.	6"/152 mm	6 cartridges	about 1,270 g	€ 1,028 (2006)
M 10 .38 Military & Police	Steel (blued)	.38 Special	4"/104 mm	6 cartridges	1,020 g	€ 666 (2010)
M 64 .38 Military & Police	Stainless steel	.38 Special	2"/51 mm	6 cartridges	about 860 g	€ 834 (2007)
M 64 .38 Military & Police	Stainless steel	.38 Special	3"/76 mm	6 cartridges	about 930 g	€ 712 (2007)
M 64 .38 Military & Police	Stainless steel	.38 Special	4"/102 mm	6 cartridges	about 990 g	€ 712 (2007)
M 67-.38 Combat Masterpiece	Stainless steel	.38 Special	4"/102 mm	6 cartridges	about 1,030 g	€ 780 (2007)
M 65 LadySmith	Stainless steel	.357 Magnum/ .38 Special	2 1/8" /54mm	6 cartridges	about 910 g	€ 775 (2004)
M 65 LadySmith	Stainless steel	.357 Magnum/ .38 Special	3"/76 mm	6 cartridges	about 910 g	€ 775 (2004)
M 65-.357 Military & Police	Stainless steel	.357 Magnum/ .38 Special	4"/102 mm	6 cartridges	about 1,040 g	€ 584 (2007)
M 66 .357 Combat Magnum	Stainless steel	.357 Magnum/ .38 Special	2 1/2" /64 mm	6 cartridges	about 910 g	€ 635 (2007)
M 66 .357 Combat Magnum	Stainless steel	.357 Magnum/ .38 Special	4"/102 mm	6 cartridges	about 1,050 g	€ 642 (2007)
M 66 .357 Combat Magnum	Stainless steel	.357 Magnum/ .38 Special	6"/150 mm	6 cartridges	1,126 g	€ 793 (2004)

* Manufacturer's information

S & W M 10 .38 Military & Police/4 inch and M 66 .357 Combat Magnum/6 inch, Technical Specifications and Prices

Manufacturer	Smith & Wesson Inc., Springfield, Massachusetts, U.S.A.	
Model	**M 10 .38 Military & Police**	**M 66 .357 Combat Magnum**
Caliber	.38 Special	.357 Magnum/.38 Special
Version	Steel, blued	Stainless steel
Weight	1,020 g	1,126 g
Cylinder capacity	6 cartridges	
Length	236 mm	284 mm
Width	36.8 mm	
Height	141 mm	146 mm
Trigger-backstrap distance	SA 75 mm/DA 86 mm	
Grip angle	110 degrees	
Grip	Combat	
Barrel	104 mm, five grooves, right twist	150 mm, five grooves, right twist
Cylinder diameter	36.8 mm	
Cylinder length	39.5 mm	41.3 mm
Cylinder gap	0.25 mm	0.20 mm
Trigger pull weight *	SA 21.41 N (2.18 kp) DA 53.57 N (5.46 kp)	SA 18.33 N (1.87 kp) DA 55.71 N (5.68 kp)
Sight length/line of sight over the barrel axis	145 mm/14 mm	198 mm/20 mm
Rear sight width/ Front sight width	3.5 mm/3.3 mm	3.3 mm/3.3 mm
Price incl. VAT	666 euros (2010)	793 euros (2004)

*TriggerScan measurements

Trigger Pull Profile [N/mm]

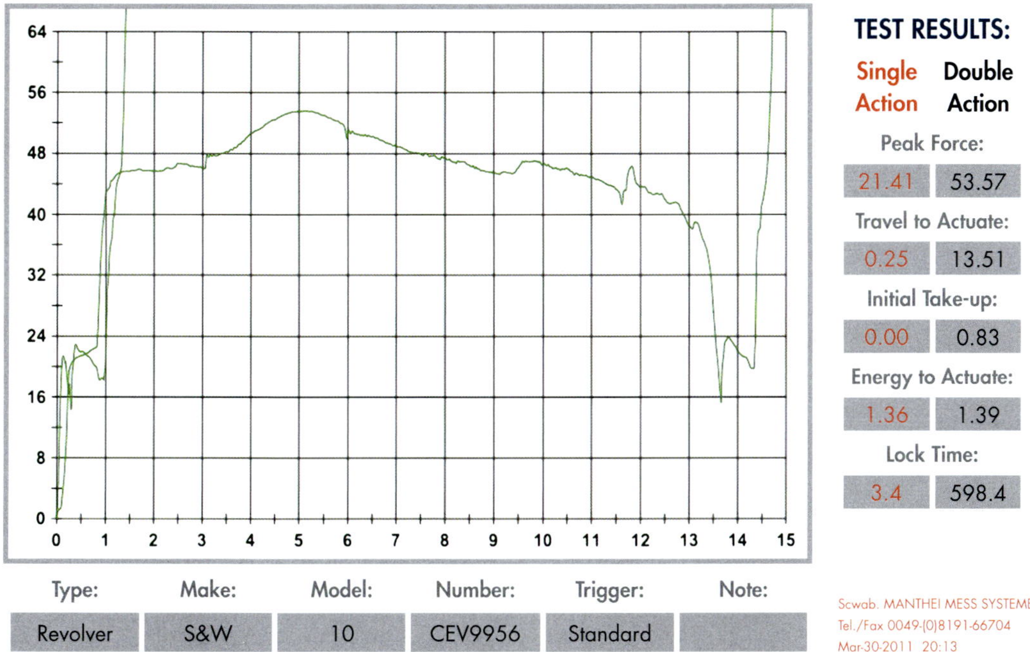

M 10-.38 Military & Police

Trigger Pull Profile [N/mm]

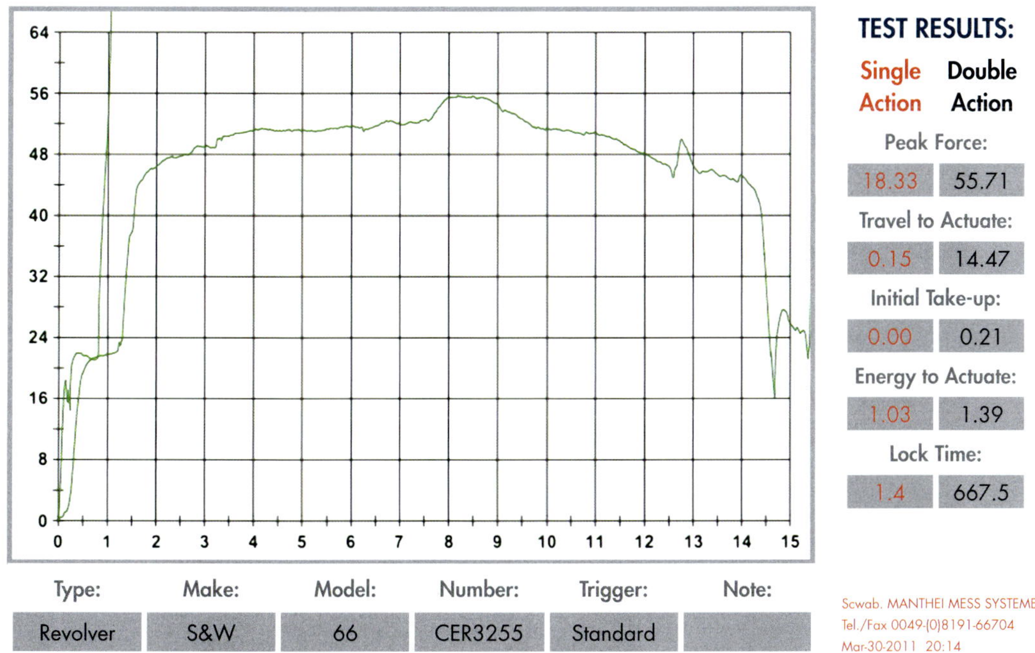

M 66-.357 Combat Magnum

L Frame Models

In 1981, Smith & Wesson closed the gap between the K and N frames. Bigger and stronger than the one, lighter and "more biddable" than the other, the new L frame offered all the best qualifications for a .357 series, and promptly ended all the discussion about their durability under the stress generated by regularly shooting powerful cartridges, and their suitability for personal use. It was the long-barreled versions, however, which created a truly sensational success in sales. Already the first-generation blued and rust-resistant six-inch M 586/686 Distinguished Combat Magnum played their role in making sure that the advanced standard models, special versions and custom guns from renowned tuners, have basically taken over target shooting today. German importers even at times placed orders for an 8 3/8 inch M 686 "for the enthusiast for excellent precision and high ballistic performance" (Wischo), as well as for the Airlites M 386 Mountain Lite (.357 Magnum/.38 Special) M 396 Mountain Lite (.44 Special), and M 296 Centennial (.44 Special), in lightweight design of scandium, aluminum, and titanium.

L Frame Models in Germany

Importers	Wischo-Jagd- und Sportwaffen GmbH & Co. KG, Erlangen Albrecht Kind GmbH (Akah), Gummersbach, Germany					
Model	**Version**	**Caliber**	**Barrel length**	**Cylinder capacity**	**Weight***	**Price (incld. VAT)**
M 296 Airlite Ti Centennial	Alu /titanium trigger DAO	.44 Special	2 1/2" /64 mm	5 cartridges	about 530 g	€ 722 (2007)
M 386 Airlite SC Mountain Lite	Scandium/ titanium (HiViz sights)	.357 Magnum/ .38 Special	3 1/8" /79 mm	7 cartridges	about 530 g	€ 1,086 (2007)
M 396 Airlite Ti Mountain Lite	Alu/titanium (HiViz sights)	.44 Special	3 1/8" /79 mm	5 cartridges	about 520 g	€ 1,072 (2007)
M 696	Stainless steel	.44 Special	3"/76 mm	5 cartridges	about 1,000 g	€ 827 (2004)
M 686 Security Special	Stainless steel (matte)	.357 Magnum/ .38 Special	3"/76 mm	6 cartridges	about 1,030 g	€ 998 (2007)
M 686 Security Special	Stainless steel (matte)	.357 Magnum/ .38 Special	4"/102 mm	6 cartridges	about 1,100 g	€ 998 (2007)
M 586 Distinguished Combat Magnum	Steel (blued)	.357 Magnum/ .38 Special	4"/102 mm 6"/152 mm	6 cartridges	about 1,190 g about 1,300 g	1,099 DM (1998)
M 586 Target Champion	Steel (blued)	.357 Magnum/ .38 Special	6"/152 mm	6 cartridges	about 1,300 g	1,298 DM (1998)

M 686 Distinguished Combat Magnum	Stainless steel	.357 Magnum/ .38 Special	2 1/2" /64 mm	6 cartridges	about 990 g	€ 811 (2007)
M 686 Distinguished Combat Magnum	Stainless steel	.357 Magnum/ .38 Special	4"/102 mm	6 cartridges	about 1,130 g	€ 827 (2007)
M 686 Distinguished Combat Magnum	Stainless steel	.357 Magnum/ .38 Special	6"/152 mm	6 cartridges	1,276 g	€ 929 (2010)
M 686 Distinguished Combat Magnum	Stainless steel	.357 Magnum/ .38 Special	8 3/8" /213 mm	6 cartridges	about 1,440 g	€ 867 (2004)
M 686 Distinguished Combat Magnum Power Port	Stainless steel	.357 Magnum/ .38 Special	6"/152 mm	6 cartridges	about 1,250 g	€ 883 (2004)
M 686 Distinguished Combat Magnum Plus	Stainless steel	.357 Magnum/ .38 Special	2 1/2" /64 mm	7 cartridges	967 g	€ 840 (2007)
M 686 Distinguished Combat Magnum Plus	Stainless steel	.357 Magnum/ .38 Special	4"/102 mm	7 cartridges	about 1,100 g	€ 841 (2007)
M 686 Distinguished Combat Magnum Plus	Stainless steel	.357 Magnum/ .38 Special	6"/152 mm	7 cartridges	about 1,220 g	€ 882 (2007)
M 686 Target Champion	Stainless steel (matte)	.357 Magnum/ .38 Special	6"/152 mm	6 cartridges	1,268 g	€ 1,119 (2010)
M 686 Target Champion DL	Stainless steel	.357 Magnum/ .38 Special	6"/152 mm	6 cartridges	about 1,250 g	€ 1,119 (2010)
M 686 Target Champion DL Match Master	Stainless steel	.357 Magnum/ .38 Special	6"/152 mm	6 cartridges	about 1,250 g	€ 1,399 (2009)
M 686 Euro Sport	Stainless steel (matte)	.357 Magnum/ .38 Special	6"/152 mm	6 cartridges	about 1,270 g	€ 922 (2004)
M 686 Euro Master	Stainless steel (matte)	.357 Magnum/ .38 Special	6"/152 mm	6 cartridges	about 1,270 g	€ 930 (2004)
M 686 Practical Champion	Stainless Steel (matte, unfluted cylinder, ramp sight)	.357 Magnum/ .38 Special	6"/152 mm	6 cartridges	about 1,270 g	€ 1,219 (2009)
M 686 Universal Champion	Stainless Steel (matte, unfluted cylinder, ramp sight)	.357 Magnum/ .38 Special	6"/152 mm	6 cartridges	varies due to additional weight	€ 1,699 (2010)
M 686 International DX	Stainless Steel (matte, unfluted cylinder)	.357 Magnum/ .38 Special	6"/152 mm	6 cartridges	about 1,270 g	€ 1,292 (2004)
M 686 "The President's"	Stainless Steel (matte, unfluted cylinder)	.357 Magnum/ .38 Special	6"/152 mm	6 cartridges	1,287 g	€ 1,329 (2010)

* Manufacturer's information

SMITH & WESSON

M 586/686 Distinguished Combat Magnum

Distinguished Combat Magnum – that stands for outstanding, the best, *the* service revolver absolute. And that is what the new L frame model was, at least as introduced in the two and a half and four-inch short versions in 1981. However, the real challenge was to make a six-inch gun that could break the dominance of the then-26-year-old Colt Python in target competition. In any case, there were enough people who would be interested in another accurate .357. There are many reasons for the rapid acceptance of the blued carbon steel model 586

The M 586 Distinguished Combat Magnum with the "medium-large" frame (Smith & Wesson) and its gradual replacement by the rust-resistant M 686, created a unique success story. Even more "Combat" as a 586, the stainless steel version developed quickly into one of the most popular guns for target shooting. Largely still in its original design, as a slightly improved Target Champion, or right from the hand of the tuner – M 686 can handle all the events that matter.

and the sustained sales success of the rust-resistant make, in all its versions. In the early 1990s, the six-inch M 686 cost just 999 DM, while for the same length Python you already had to lay out 1,698 DM. In 2004, Frankonia offered the six-inch M 686-6 for 835 euros and asked 1,639 euros for the four- to six-inch special model, still only available as the Python Elite from the Colt Custom Shop. In terms of externals, what makes an impression is the elegance: the result of enhancing the classic concept of the gun's appearance with the muzzle-length underlug and successfully integrating it into the front view. In practice, the L frame models benefit from their handiness, retained despite the heavy frame, the

larger cylinder, and the higher pre-loading capacity, compared to the K series. And technically, its old, but by no means obsolete, trigger mechanism, means that this revolver can be adapted to just about any requirements. Nothing can be ruled out where the accessories trade is concerned, and as to the tuning gunsmith, these revolvers, no matter how much they have been developed, represent a perpetual construction site.

The L frame models received their standard alterations mostly at the same time as the other series did. Smith & Wesson always dealt with this process with great care, so as not to disturb the already successful design. To identify them, the generations were given consecutive numbers; for example, a 5 or 6 was added to the weapon type. The first three generations were still drop forged, square or round butt frames, that could take, depending on the version, traditionally shaped wooden grip panels, wooden target or combat grips, or soft rubber grip in the style of the one-piece Hogue monogrip. The well-known flexible ignition on the hammer transmits the ignition impulse; in the cylinder, the ejector rod profiled guide and two "indigenous" guide pins take care of centering the ejector star and making the cylinder rotate as uniformly as possible. More minor differences include the covered frame surfaces, that also could sometimes mean that the finishing touches could be omitted in respect to cartridge case friction on the breech face, and the not initially fixed ignition bushing.

When Smith & Wesson shifted production to numerically controlled machine tools in the early-1990s, this was applied in 1993 to the recently enhanced three- and four-inch M 686 Security Special and the six-inch M 686 Target Champion fourth L frame generation: the frames, only manufactured with round butts, were milled from a solid block, and the catches on the back of the cylinder were replaced by a self-centering ejector star. However, the safe entry of the star in the form-fit relief-milled cylinder back required more play than the pins. In addition, these pieces featured an overall higher standard of workmanship in the non-polished, finely finished or matte peened frame surfaces, a rounded sight base, two additional threaded bores in the frame bridge for mounting alternative target devices, and a spring-loaded pin in the front lock plate and crane strain screw.

Transition to MIM Technology

In the search for more efficient production methods, in the late-1990s Smith & Wesson turned to MIM technology. Metal injection molding is a modern metal injection casting process, in which the powdered metal and binder are injected into the mold, are hardened or sintered under high temperature, and can be removed from the mold practically as a finished part. This technique was used for the fifth-generation L frame models in 1998, and, thanks to good testing, are still in stock – production costs were again lowered for the relevant components, and they showed no adverse effects during the probation period. The new series' frames feature integrated "tear drops"; previously, a pin was inserted in this place to prevent the swung-out cylinder from slipping by the crane. Other features include the rebounding firing pin mounted in the frame, the delicately injection-molded essential parts of the trigger mechanism, and the less angular cylinder release. In addition, the inner barrel profile is not created by drawing, but by the ECD (Electrochemical Decharging) method. The twist length remains 476 mm.

MIM hammers and triggers differ in appearance from the forged, milled and hardened predecessors, due to their accurate casting mold, a partially recessed hammer edges, a hammer striking surface instead of moveable ignition, the loosely inserted hammer lifter, the MTM track linked to the hammer, and the deep chamfer of the trigger. There are also major differences in how they function. The TriggerScan diagrams demonstrate the weaker setting of the M 586-4 (BSR 8786) trigger pull weight of 12.0 kp N/1.22 in single action and 32.32 N/3.29 kp in double action, with the specific, almost horizontal double action profile between the third and twelfth millimeters of the travel to actuate (1.6 mm to 6.5 mm: cylinder rotation; 6.5 to 7 mm: cylinder stop engages; 10 to 11 mm: catch transfer; 12.1 mm: hammer drops) and the uniform cylinder rotation over all six positions. In contrast, the standard M 686-6 (CFH 1932) shows a single-action trigger pull weight of 19.84 N/2.02 kp. The double action profile reaches its maximum of 53.78 N/5.49 kp in the middle of cylinder rotation (at 5 mm), rises again at the catch transfer to 46.24 N/4.72 kp (at 10.4 mm) and first falls short of the 40 Newton mark just before the drop of the hammer (at 13.5 mm). Beyond this, measurements from chamber to chamber vary between the beginning of the cylinder rotation and the fall of the hammer by up to ten Newton.

Without in fact disputing the Colt Python's 25 meter best performance of a 25 millimeter group each with .357 Geco (10.2 g SJ FP) and Lapua (9.7 g CEPP) factory, the M 586 achieved 31 with the .357 Lapua (9.7 g CEPP) and the M 686 achieved 27 millimeters with the .357 Winchester (10.2 g SJ FP). The Distinguished Combat Magnum's real strength is its overall good ammunition compatibility.

The seventh shot in the cylinder is a plus for the model. This doesn't give the M 686 Distinguished Combat Magnum Plus much extra capital for target shooting, however, since usually only five rounds are loaded. This model comes in the same barrel lengths as the six-shooter.

LAPUA
.357 MAG.
LAPUA
.357 MAG.
LAPUA
.357 MAG.
LAPUA
.357 MAG.
LAPUA
.357 MAG.
LAPUA
.357 MAG.
LAPUA
.357 MAG.
TRADE
MARK

M 686 Target Champion

The M 686 Target Champion is probably the best-known L frame special model in Germany. Ex-importer Wischo offered the refined standard model, with peened finish, target hammer and trigger, Millett adjustable sights, interchangeable front sight and Nill target grip.

Standard or Target Champion? – No question for performance oriented shooters. The Target model, which costs just 190 euros more, offers, besides the typical TC-look with satin finish and generous barrel, wider target-shooting style hammer and trigger, hallmark Nill walnut wood grip panels with finger grooves, a Millett adjustable sight, and a high contrast front sight. The grip alone, which are suitable for both-handed shooting without adjustable hand rests, and the undercut target front sight, are worth the extra cost in terms of shooting performance. In dimmer light conditions, the latter literally puts the standard ramp front sight with orange plastic insert in the shade.

In substance, the M 686 Target Champion corresponds to the standard version. In contrast to an M 686 "Super Target Champion" from the Smith & Wesson Performance Center, with its handpicked and carefully overhauled standard parts. The Target Champion represents the state of the art for mass production; there were not even any modest improvements in the trigger

Target-shooting features: Millett sight and target front sight (left). Rear and front sight of the original correspond to the standard sights for practical use.

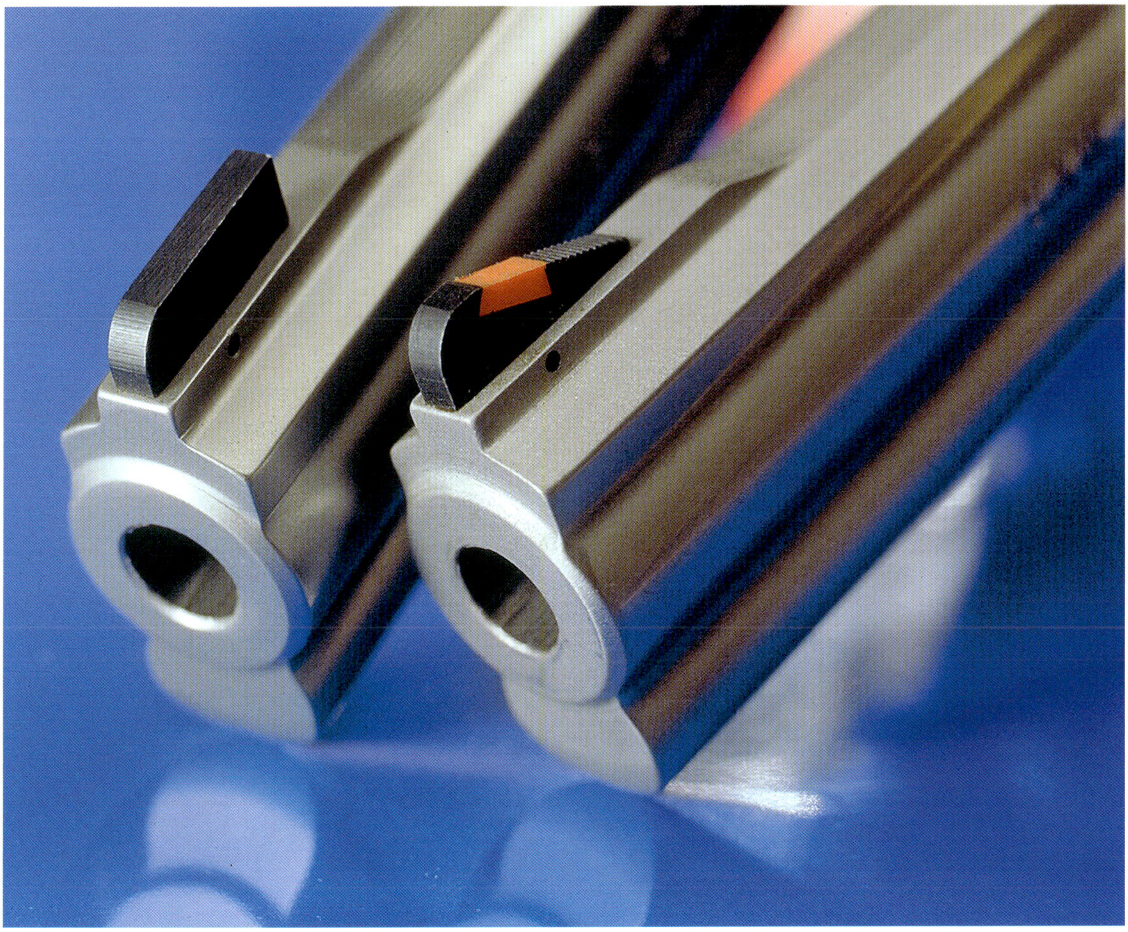

mechanism. The deviations in the pull weight profiles only attest to the adjustment and manufacturing tolerances.

The basic first large-caliber Target Champion still corresponded to the M 686-3, with forged frame and guide pins for the ejector star. These early makes bore the lettering ".357 Target Champion" on the lock plate and the company logo offset to the left under the cylinder release. In its final appearance, this model became the target-shooting spin-off of the 1993 standards, as M 686-4 in the continuing CNC production. As a concession to the enthusiasts for mirror-polished blued carbon steel – on which the laser engravings worked particularly well – there was a companion matte finish M 586 Target Champion, until the 5th Series was launched in 1998. Versions with other features include the M 686 Target Champion DL, with fine finished surface, and the M 686 Target Champion DL Match Master, with overhauled trigger mechanism, symmetric Nill walnut wood grip panels, TXT sight from LPA and two-level ramp sight.

M 686 "The President's"

"The President's" – a special model for the commander-in-chief of the U.S. land, sea and air forces for self-defense? This is what the dedication and presentation seem to suggest. But importer Wischo knows better: "An unusual weapon for shooters who love something special." With that, he means the titanium treatment of visually outstanding components: the unfluted cylinder, cylinder release, ejector rod and visible parts of the trigger mechanism. Especially attractive – if in fact it meets the customer's taste at all – is the imitation gold, although only on the mirror-polished cylinder, the smoothed ejector rod and the fluted slide. On the trigger and hammer, the "natural state" also-coated casting seams and other irregularities are less pleasing.

"The President's" is a Wischo special model, with its presidential outfitting mainly expressed in the "zero carat gold" gilding of the unfluted cylinder and other parts. The Target Champion Sight and special Nill fine wood grip panels round out the unusual features.

S.&W. 357 MAGNUM
CFJ0451

While the cylinder is sufficient for its presidential aspirations …

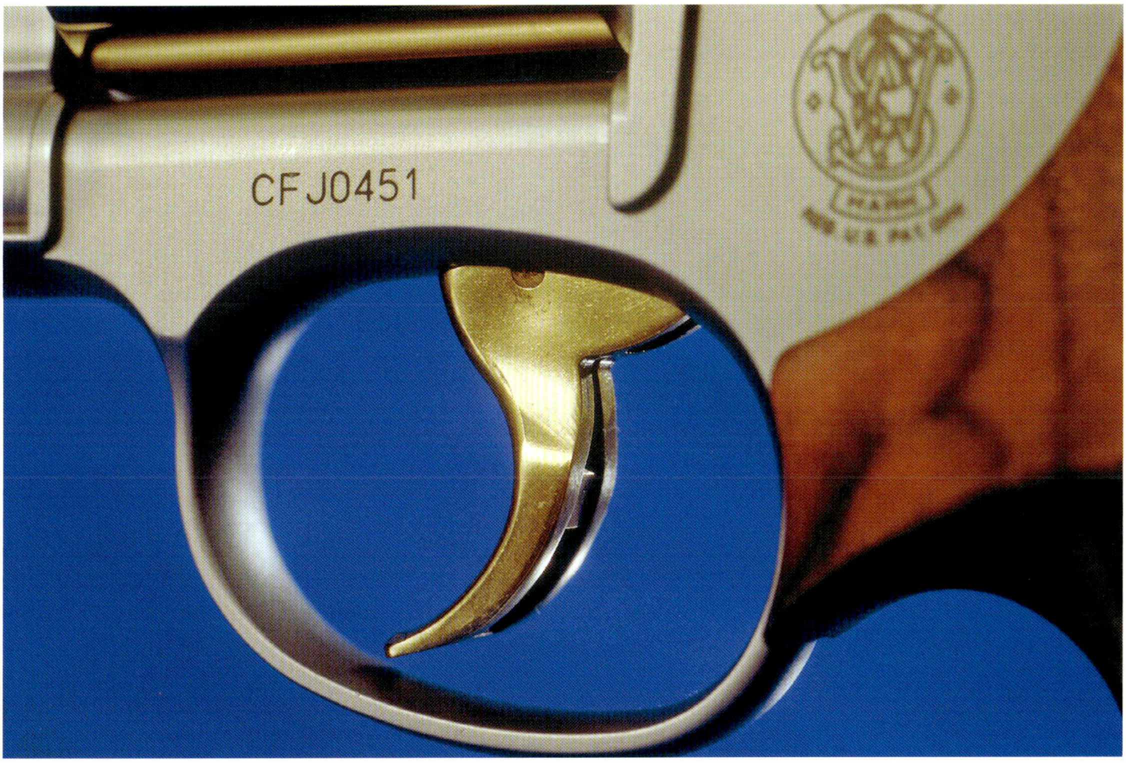

… under the covering, trigger and hammer are rather more folksy types.

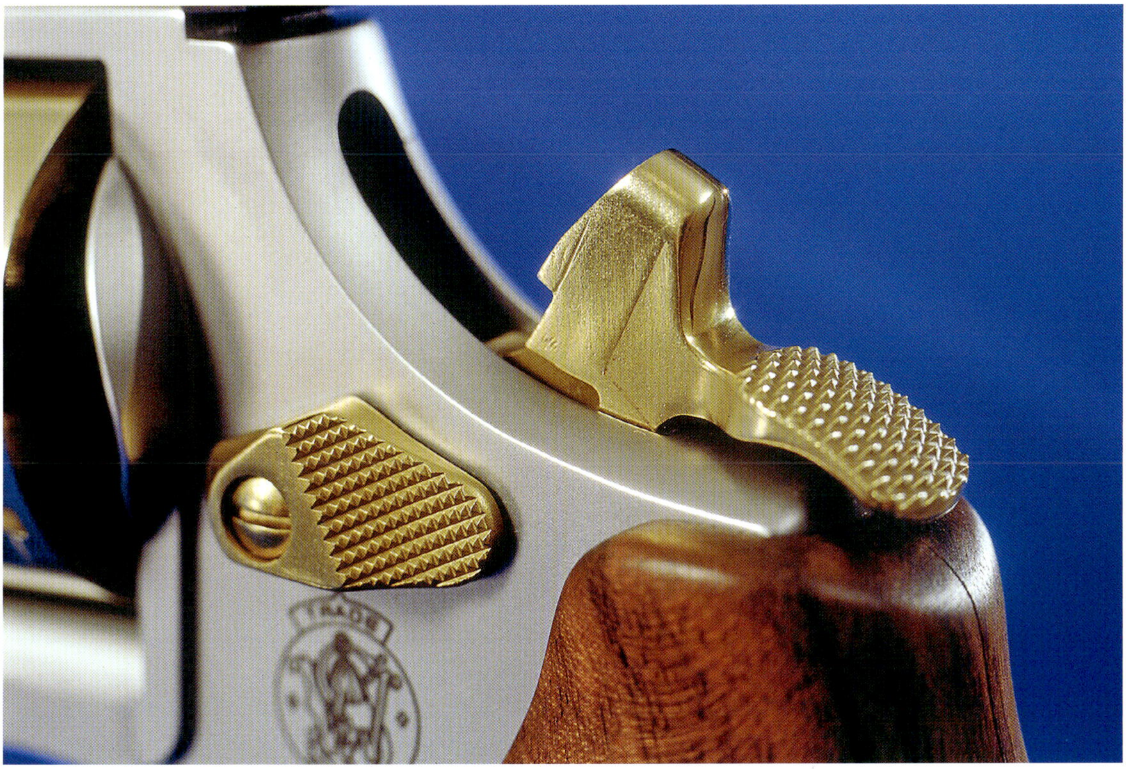

Structurally, the presidential six incher is a fifth or sixth generation Target Champion with peened finish, laser inscription, Millett sight, dowelled target sight and comparable trigger mechanism action – the whole "easier" adjustment is faced with a higher pull weight when transferring the catch in double action. Symmetrical Nill fine wood grip panels with finger grooves and checkering complement this fine millennial creation.

M 686 Distinguished Combat Magnum Plus

Taurus started it all. Loosely after the motto: "One more shot in the cylinder can never be too much," in 1995, the Brazilian arms manufacturer created, using frame and cylinder of the .44 Magnum revolver M 44 CP, the first mass produced "seven-shooter" in caliber. 357 Magnum. The firepower of the model 607 should especially be available where a larger cylinder capacity can also be used, to tap additional market shares. Smith & Wesson responded immediately, and in the same year brought out another special model of the versatile M 686 Distinguished Combat Magnum, with a "plus" for the seventh cartridge. Whereupon, Taurus again took the offensive in 1996, with the M 608 eight-shooter.

This meant that both companies had reached the maximum capacity of their basic models. In the 39.6 millimeter diameter L frame cylinder, having seven 9.75 millimeter bores meant "thinning out" the chamber partitions from 3.2 to 1.6 millimeters, while at the same time easing the burden on the 2.2 millimeter thick outer walls by the necessary addition of 1.2 millimeter deep locking grooves between the chambers. The offset is due to the uneven division.

Since cylinder rotation each time of 51.4 instead of 60 degrees, neither affects the sequence in the trigger mechanism nor operation of the cylinder stop, the M 686 Distinguished Combat Magnum Plus concept is expressed, so to speak, only in the modified cylinder and matching ejector with seven ratchets. All other details conform to the standard: the frame, crane, trigger mechanism, alternate barrel lengths of 3, 4 and 6 inches, the "roulette" sight, the dowelled ramp front sight and the Hogue monogrip. The cylinder rotates in a very uniform movement across all seven stations.

Smith & Wesson M 686 Distinguished Combat Magnum/ 2 1/2 and 6 inches, Technical Specifications and Prices

Manufacturer	Smith & Wesson Inc., Springfield, Massachusetts, USA			
Model	**M 686 Distinguished Combat Magnum**	**M 686 Target Champion**	**M 686 "The President's"**	**M 686 Distinguished Combat Magnum Plus**
Caliber	.357 Magnum/.38 Special			
Version	Stainless steel			
Weight	1,276 g	1,268 g	1,287 g	967 g
Cylinder capacity	6 cartridges	6 cartridges	6 cartridges	7 cartridges
Length	287 mm	293 mm	292 mm	188 mm
Width	39.6 mm			
Height	152 mm	152 mm	150 mm	152 mm
Trigger-backstrap distance	SA 72 mm DA 83 mm	SA 76 mm DA 87 mm	SA 75 mm DA 86 mm	SA 72 mm DA 83 mm
Grip angle	110 degrees			
Grip/grip panels	Hogue monogrip	Nill wood grip panels	Nill wood grip panels	Hogue monogrip
Barrel	152 mm, five grooves right twist	152 mm, five grooves right twist	152 mm, five grooves right twist	64 mm, five groves right twist
Cylinder diameter	39.6 mm			
Cylinder length	41.3 mm			
Cylinder gap	0.15 mm	0.20mm	0.15 mm	0.15 mm
Trigger pull weight*	SA 19.84 N/2.02 kp DA 53.78 N/5.49 kp	SA 23.29 N/2,38 kp DA 52.91 N/5.40 kp	SA 20.38 N/2.08 kp DA 49.62 N/5.06 kp	SA 20.92 N/2.13 DA 51.02 N/5.20 kp
Sight length/ line of sight over the barrel axis	198 mm/22 mm	192 mm/20 mm	192 mm/20 mm	110 mm/22 mm
Rear sight width/ front sight width	3.3 mm/3.3 mm			
Price incl. VAT	929 euros (2010)	1,119 euros (2010)	1,329 euros (2010)	840 euros (2007)

*TriggerScan measurements

Trigger Pull Profile [N/mm]

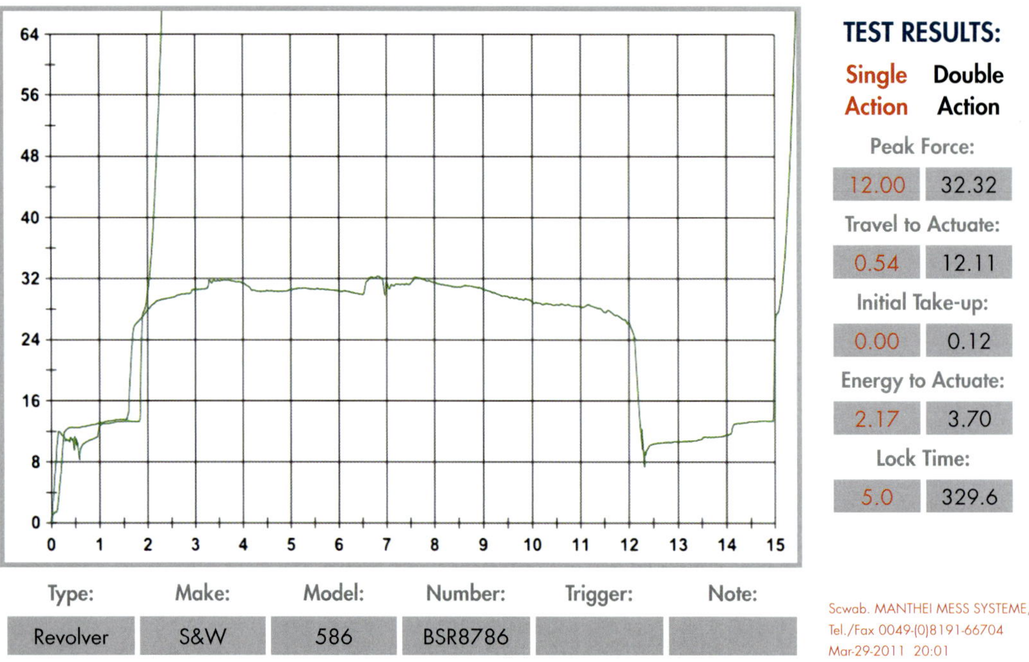

M 586 Distinguished Combat Magnum with Wilson Combat springs.

Trigger Pull Profile [N/mm]

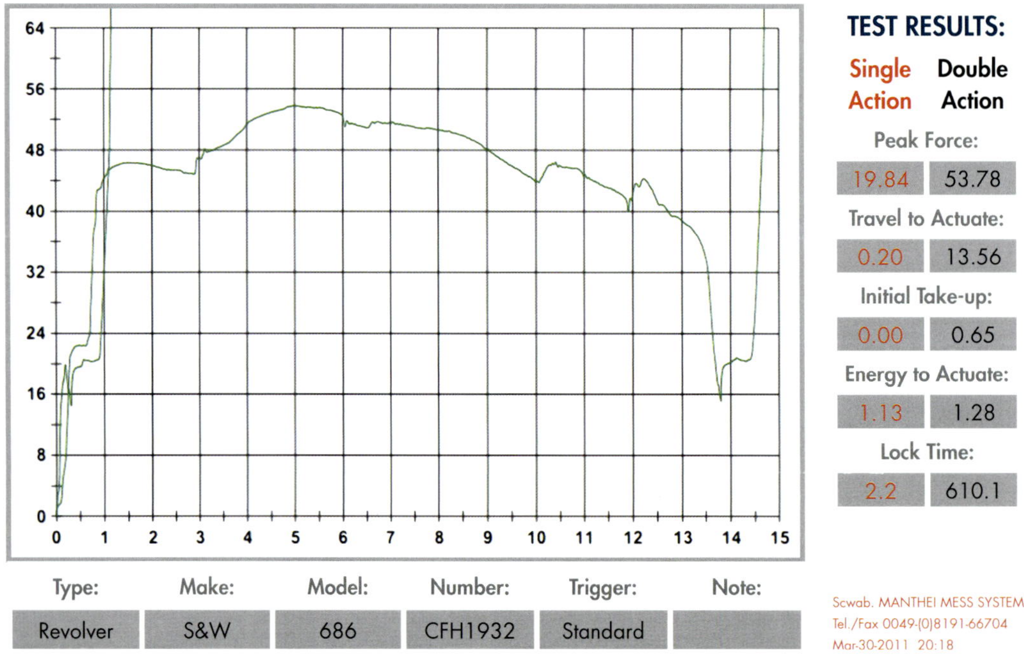

M 686 Distinguished Combat Magnum.

L Frame Models

Trigger Pull Profile [N/mm]

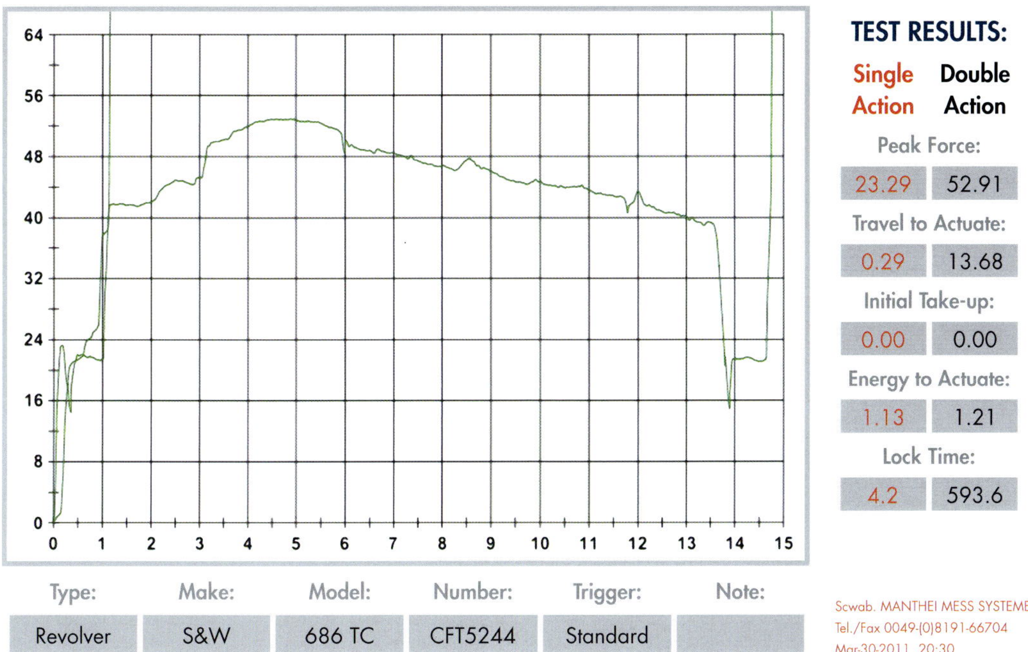

TEST RESULTS:

	Single Action	Double Action
Peak Force:	23.29	52.91
Travel to Actuate:	0.29	13.68
Initial Take-up:	0.00	0.00
Energy to Actuate:	1.13	1.21
Lock Time:	4.2	593.6

Type:	Make:	Model:	Number:	Trigger:	Note:
Revolver	S&W	686 TC	CFT5244	Standard	

Scwab. MANTHEI MESS SYSTEME,
Tel./Fax 0049-(0)8191-66704
Mar-30-2011 20:30

M 686 Target Champion

Trigger Pull Profile [N/mm]

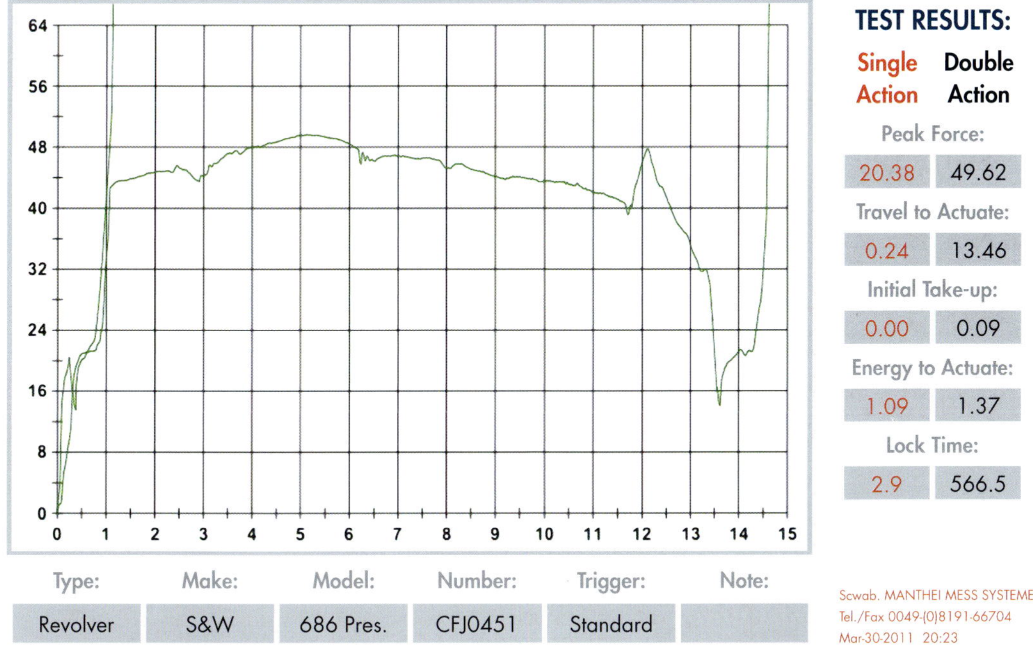

TEST RESULTS:

	Single Action	Double Action
Peak Force:	20.38	49.62
Travel to Actuate:	0.24	13.46
Initial Take-up:	0.00	0.09
Energy to Actuate:	1.09	1.37
Lock Time:	2.9	566.5

Type:	Make:	Model:	Number:	Trigger:	Note:
Revolver	S&W	686 Pres.	CFJ0451	Standard	

Scwab. MANTHEI MESS SYSTEME,
Tel./Fax 0049-(0)8191-66704
Mar-30-2011 20:23

M 686 "The President's"

N Frame Models

By 1908, twelve years after the .38 Hand Ejector First Model, the .44 Hand Ejector Model New Century was setting new standards. This first large frame, with the recently (1907) introduced .44 Special cartridge, was the result of the compelling momentum to produce ever larger calibers, and launched another series. The basic idea of "everything one size bigger" was enough, to keep the next frame which was developed (the N frame) in the "large" Magnum class. A comparison of K and N frames shows more than just the reinforcement of the larger frame required for the caliber and the appropriate crane. The cylinder also, because of the holes, required entirely different dimensions for its supporting parts, and, of necessity, the trigger mechanism could not be transferred as is, due to the size of the components, although the same design principles were used for the N frame version. Altogether – of course including barrel, sights, and grip – the resulting

All N frame models using shorter cartridges are designed with the same length compensation used in the other series: the barrel, which protrudes far down the threading, bridges the large cylinder gap from the frame yoke. The Target Champion version of the rust-resistant .357 model 627 has the matte finish typical for Wischo specials, and also features the customary Millett sight, as well as a Nill shaped grip for one-handed shooting.

weapon is bigger, heavier, and not as easy to wield. Smith & Wesson's Triple Lock, initially considered necessary to lock the cylinder with an additional safety on the crane, was abandoned by 1915. The caliber range was once from .38 to .455; it currently includes 10 mm/.40, .45 ACP, .357/.38 and .44 Mag./.44 Special.

The new grip's good qualities had already enhanced the .45 Hand Ejector, better known as the 1917 Army Model, a .45 caliber ACP military revolver which was manufactured in large quantities. Smith & Wesson had only to adjust the cylinder length and barrel outlet on the frame to the rimless pistol cartridge, and was ready to deliver its counterpart to the Colt .45 Automatic Government Model of 1911, with two crescent clips, to the U.S. forces. A short cylinder and a barrel cut to a correspond length, also earmarked the models 27 and 28 Highway Patrolman for the .357 Magnum cartridge introduced in 1935. However, the large frames did not always make things so easy with the "small" Magnums. Other examples of the liberal use of N frames include the follow-up military revolvers M 21 and M 22 in caliber .44 Special, and .45 ACP (1950), the Target spin-off M 24 in both calibers, and the Target Model 25 in .45 ACP (1955).

That same year, in a successful next step, Smith & Wesson and Remington brought the M 29 and the .44 Magnum cartridge together. "Probably no handgun cartridge has received more publicity and attention than the .44 Magnum," munitions expert Dave Andrews later asserted in *Speer Reloading Manual.* The weapon that first shot this 1,300-joule power-dwarf excited the same amount of attention. In 1964, the M 57 appeared as a companion of the less-successful .41 Remington Magnum cartridge. In 1979, the stainless steel M 629 began to compete with the blued M 29; since 1988, the M 629 Classic has featured the already past-due full lug. For a while, there was the eight-inch M 629 Classic DX, made specifically for target shooters, with guaranteed maximal group of one inch at twenty-five yards from the shooting machine, and five interchangeable front sights.

In 1955, Remington and Smith & Wesson developed, virtually simultaneously, the strongest .44 Magnum revolver cartridge for a long time, and the carbon steel large-frame Model 29 designed for it. Fourteen years after the revolutionary M 60, since 1979, the also constantly evolving stainless steel M 629 has been on the market – a classic with its short ejector rod housing, the so-called half lug.

The resounding success of the L frame models led Smith & Wesson in 1988 to issue a second .44 as the M 29/629 Classic with full underlug, probably not only because of its better balance. Its successful looks have certainly also played a role. The CL comes with a full range of features, with barrel lengths from 4 to 12 inches.

N Frame Models in Germany

Importers	Wischo-Jagd- und Sportwaffen GmbH & Co. KG, Erlangen, Germany Albrecht Kind GmbH (Akah), Gummersbach, Germany					
Model	**Version**	**Caliber**	**Barrel length**	**Cylinder capacity**	**Weight***	**Price (incld. VAT)**
M 610	Stainless steel	10 mm auto./ .40 S & W	4"/102 mm	6 cartridges	about 1,280 g	€ 1,108 (2004)
M 625	Stainless steel (matte)	.45 ACP	5"/127 mm	6 cartridges	about 1,275 g	€ 983 (2010)
M 627 Target Champion	Stainless steel (matte, unfluted cylinder)	.357 Magnum/ .38 Special	6 "/152 mm	6 cartridges	1,430 g	€ 1,299 (2010)
M 29	Steel (blued)	.44 Magnum/ .44 Special	6 1/2"/165 mm	6 cartridges	about 1,375 g	€ 1,249 (2010)
M 629	Stainless steel	.44 Magnum/ .44 Special	4"/102 mm	6 cartridges	about 1,180 g	€ 970 (2005)
M 629	Stainless steel	.44 Magnum/ .44 Special	6"/149 mm	6 cartridges	1,277 g	€ 1,039 (2010)
M 629	Stainless steel	.44 Magnum/ .44 Special	8 3/8"/213 mm	6 cartridges	about 1,400 g	1,246 DM (1996)
M 629 Classic	Stainless steel	.44 Magnum/ .44 Special	5"/127 mm	6 cartridges	about 1,380 g	€ 999 (2007)
M 629 Classic	Stainless steel	.44 Magnum/ .44 Special	6 "/152 mm	6 cartridges	about 1,390 g	€ 935 (2006)
M 629 Classic	Stainless steel	.44 Magnum/ .44 Special	6 1/2"/165 mm	6 cartridges	1,370 g	€ 1,039 (2010)
M 629 Classic	Stainless steel	.44 Magnum/ .44 Special	8- 3/8"/213 mm	6 cartridges	about 1,500 g	€ 1,086 (2003)
M 629 Classic Power Port	Stainless steel	.44 Magnum/ .44 Special	6 1/2"/165 mm	6 cartridges	about 1,550 g	€ 1,021 (2005)
M 629 Classic DX	Stainless steel	.44 Magnum/ .44 Special	6 1/2"/165 mm	6 cartridges	about 1,400 g	€ 999 (2006)
M 629 Classic DX	Stainless steel	.44 Magnum/ .44 Special	8"/203 mm	6 cartridges	about 1,480 g	€ 1389 (2003)
M 629 Classic Champion	Stainless steel (matte, unfluted cylinder)	.44 Magnum/ .44 Special	6 "/152 mm	6 cartridges	about 1,400 g	€ 1,369 (2010)
M 629 Competitor	Stainless steel (matte)	.44 Magnum/ .44 Special	6 "/152 mm	6 cartridges	about 1,500 g	€ 1,656 (2003)
M 629 Extreme Hunter	Stainless steel (matte)	.44 Magnum/ .44 Special	12"/305 mm	6 cartridges	about 1,700 g	€ 1,654 (2007)

* Manufacturer's information

Smith-Wesson M 627 Target Champion/6 inches, M 629/6 inches and 629 Classic M/6 1/2 inches Technical Specifications and Prices

Manufacturer	Smith & Wesson Inc., Springfield, Massachusetts, USA		
Model	M 627 Target Champion	M 629	M 629 Classic
Caliber	.357 Magnum/ .38 Special	.44 Magnum/.44 Special	.44 Magnum/.44 Special
Version	Stainless steel		
Weight	1,430 g	1,277 g	1,370 g
Cylinder capacity	6 cartridges		
Length	293 mm	288 mm	305 mm
Width	43.5 mm		
Height	154 mm	157 mm	157 mm
Trigger-backstrap distance	SA 77 mm DA 88 mm	SA 72 mm DA 83 mm	SA 72 mm DA 83 mm
Grip angle	110 degrees		
Grip/grip panels	Nill grip	Combat	Fine wood
Barrel	152 mm, five grooves, right twist	149 mm, five grooves, right twist	165 mm, five grooves, right twist
Cylinder diameter	43.5 mm		
Cylinder length	40 mm	43.3 mm	43.3 mm
Cylinder gap	0.12 mm	0.15 mm	0.15 mm
Trigger pull weight*	SA 16.78 N/1.71 kp DA 61.06 N/6.23 kp	SA 21.78 N/2.22 kp DA 66.64 N/6.80 kp	SA 23.84 N/2.43 kp DA 54.38 N/5.55 kp
Sight length/ line of sight over the barrel axis	192 mm/20 mm	200 mm/23 mm	215 mm/23 mm
Rear sight width/ front sight width	3.3 mm/3.3 mm		
Price incl. VAT	1,299 euros (2010)	1,039 euros (2010)	1,039 euros (2010)

*TriggerScan measurements

Trigger Pull Profile [N/mm]

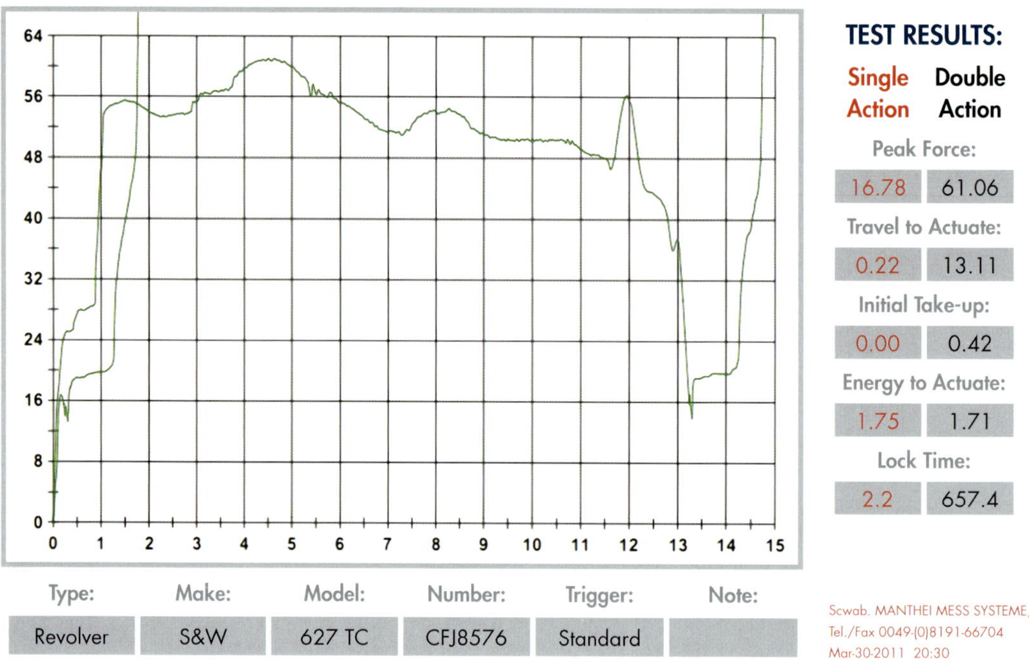

	Single Action	Double Action
Peak Force:	16.78	61.06
Travel to Actuate:	0.22	13.11
Initial Take-up:	0.00	0.42
Energy to Actuate:	1.75	1.71
Lock Time:	2.2	657.4

Type:	Make:	Model:	Number:	Trigger:	Note:
Revolver	S&W	627 TC	CFJ8576	Standard	

M 627 Target Champion

Trigger Pull Profile [N/mm]

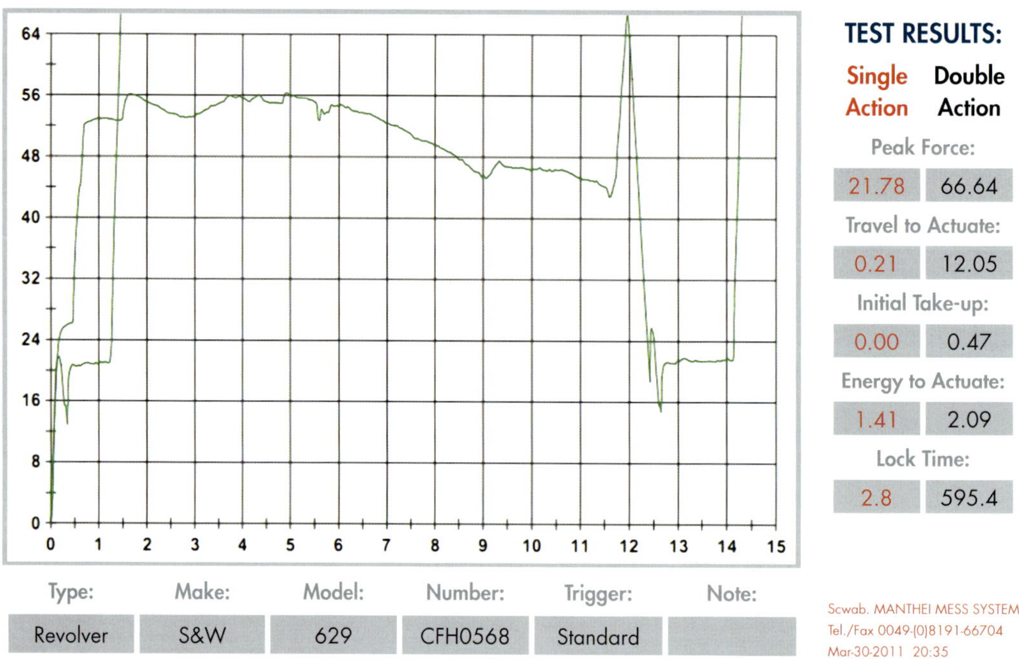

	Single Action	Double Action
Peak Force:	21.78	66.64
Travel to Actuate:	0.21	12.05
Initial Take-up:	0.00	0.47
Energy to Actuate:	1.41	2.09
Lock Time:	2.8	595.4

Type:	Make:	Model:	Number:	Trigger:	Note:
Revolver	S&W	629	CFH0568	Standard	

M 629

Trigger Pull Profile [N/mm]

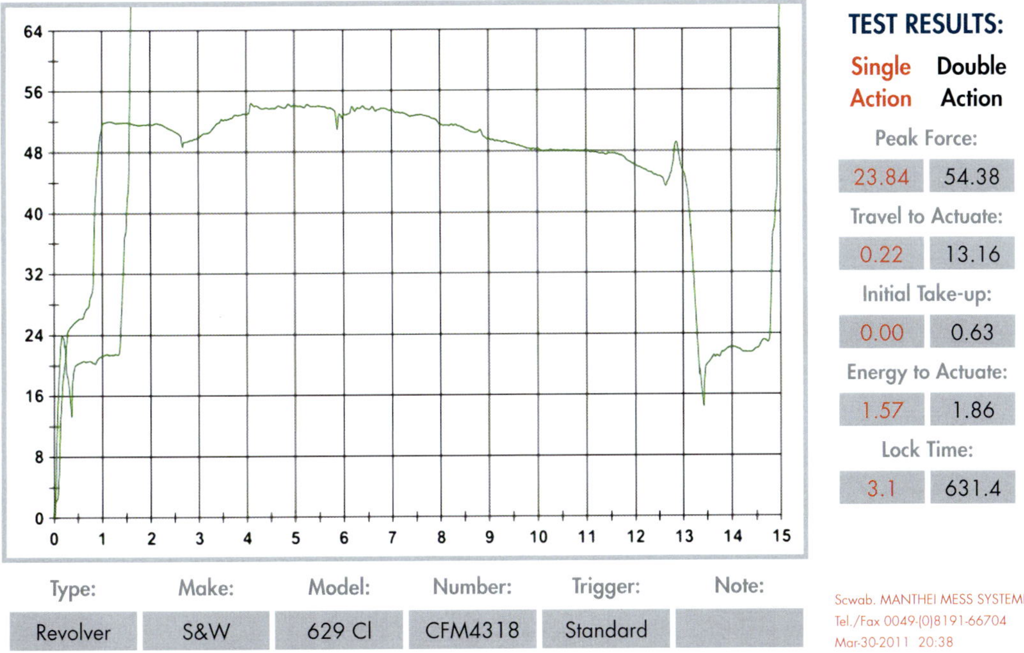

M 629 Classic

J Frame Models

As a weapon for self-defense or hunting, the short-barreled revolver can still compete successfully with the pistol. But not only professionals and hunters appreciate the special qualities of this revolver, which is less than two or three inches: The compact design, low weight, rapid fire-readiness, the high efficiency especially of the .357 Magnum, the safety, and its total reliability. "Snubnoses" and related models also have a lot of fascination for target shooters; the BDS (Bund Deutscher Sportschützen) [German Sports Shooters Association] and international associations all sponsor appropriate events. Since the introduction of the I frame models around 1950, Smith & Wesson has served its clientele with the J frame models for stronger calibers. The ammunition-related differences in the dimensions and cylinder capacity (five to eight shots), are self-evident.

Contrary to the practice of upgrading a series' basic model into a special model using tighter tolerances, alternate finishes, and special feature details, in the J frame models Smith & Wesson offers in real diversity of types. A revolver for your handbag, such as the Ladysmith (with an M frame, still written as LadySmith until 1921); for concealed carry, such as for bodyguards; for the fast draw holster, such as the Chief's Special; or for hunters, such as the Airlite Ti SC Kit Gun – they all differ in material, design, and handling. Smith & Wesson's

Airlite, for example, is a revolver as with light-metal frame and steel cylinder; the Airlite Ti, includes even lighter models with light-metal frame and titanium cylinder. Even within the Ti series, there are marked differences: three of the 340-gram lightweights – the l 7/8 inch M 332 Centennial in caliber .32 H&R Magnum (.32 Harrington & Richardson Magnum), M 342/342 PD Centennial in .38 Special, and M 340 Centennial in .357 Magnum/.38 Special – equipped with a solid frame. The hammer cover and the sights, a milled in rectangular rear sight in the frame bridge and a ramp front sight, are designed to ensure that

Ms. Förstner [Forester] is neither a forester nor a hunter. But the Ladysmith suits her just right.

the weapon can be drawn unhindered. The Centennial's trigger mechanism is Double Action Only. Instead of a hammer with spur and the typical flat spring, Smith & Wesson used a striker (hammer) flattened on the top with rod-guided coil spring. A spring-loaded firing pin in the frame replaces the movable hammer pin, and the hammer block linked to the slide was eliminated. The hammer reset and short length of the firing pin were retained as safety mechanisms – because a Centennial certainly cannot fall on the hammer. The other Ti models have the usual single- and double-action trigger mechanism.

In contrast to the K frame Model 65 Lady Smith.357 Magnum, the M 36 LS, as a .38, is based on the smaller J frame. The polished fine wood grip panels are especially ladylike.

The first Smith & Wesson in stainless steel was not the M 60 Chief's Special Magnum. That fame and honor go only to the 1965 Chief's in .38 Special.

The 1 7/8 to 2 inch .38 Airweight models M 637 Chief's Special, M 638 Bodyguard and M 642 Centennial also feature a light metal frame and the choice between open or enclosed hammer. Compared with the single and double action Chief's and the single-action only Centennial, the Bodyguard offers yet another possibility: if necessary, you can cock the slightly protruding (shrouded) hammer with your thumb.

For this, the frame back was cut out and contains an almost "normal" hammer, which is snappily fluted on its spur. This is cocked by the same mainspring used in the Centennial, fired in the frame with the firing pin, and secured by the entire

safety system which the original trigger mechanism featured. The Airweights weigh between 420 to 430 grams All other J frame models are stainless steel weapons, like the .357.

640 Centennial Magnum and M 649 Magnum Bodyguard. Or the convential successors to the 1950 Chief's Special, such as the M 36 Lady Smith in caliber .38 Special and the M 60 Chief's Special Magnum in .357 Magnum/.38 Special. In 1965, still as a .38, the Chief's sparked the production of a wave of stainless steel revolvers. In Vietnam, it is reported (Boorman), GIs would even swap alcohol for the $85 stainless steel model.

M 60: Basically, it has the well-known trigger mechanism. This was only "shrunk" for the J frame, and has a coil spring instead of the normal flat spring. Since the introduction of MIM injection molding technology, a frame-bound firing pin has replaced the hammer pin.

Compact and just for general use: at left, the M 649 Bodyguard Magnum with shrouded hammer; at right, the DAO model Centennial 640 Magnum.

If there were the term "semi-DAO," it would fit here: Double Action Only – and, if necessary, single action too. In addition – and this is the intention – the Bodyguard fits smoothly in a bodyguard's hand.

The "mini" hammer spur barely shows on the Bodyguard trigger mechanism.

Uncompromising: Double Action Only – and that's it. At second glance, the Centennial differs from the Bodyguard with a frame hump to accommodate the higher lock plate screw.

In the Centennial, the hammer reset is enough. The additional impact and drop safety from the hammer block on the trigger was eliminated.

Titanium, a tough and lightweight material for high-stress parts, such as the connecting rods in the earlier Porsche TAG Turbo Grand Prix Motor, has long since arrived in automotive technology. This exotic metal has also become increasingly important in civilian weaponry – such as for Race Guns for IPSC shooting. Smith & Wesson combined cylinders from a titanium alloy with a frames made of aluminum alloy to make the Airlite Ti models. In the photo: the partially black anodized M 337 Airlite Ti PD in .38 Special + P caliber.

M 337 Airlite Ti PD en bloc and in detail: The five-shot .38 weighs just 312 grams.

Titanium cylinder with maxed out capacity.

Rear sight in the frame bridge, pinned ramp sight in the barrel shroud.

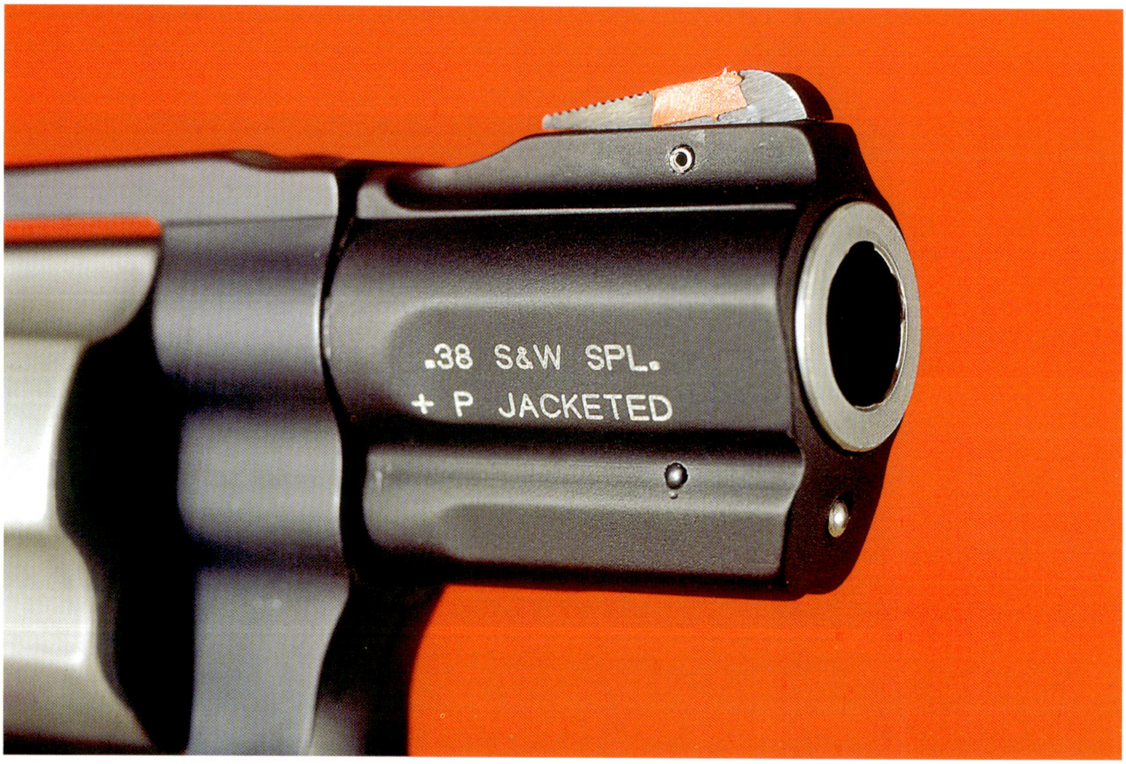

J Frame Models in Germany

Importers	Wischo-Jagd- und Sportwaffen GmbH & Co. KG, Erlangen, Germany Albrecht Kind GmbH (Akah), Gummersbach, Germany					
Model	**Version**	**Caliber**	**Barrel length**	**Cylinder capacity**	**Weight***	**Price (incld. VAT)**
M 317 Airlite	LM/steel	.22 LR	1 7/8"/48mm	8 cartridges	about 300 g	€ 725 (2007)
M 317 Airlite	LM/steel	.22 LR	3 "/76 mm	8 cartridges	about 380 g	€ 793 (2007)
M 331 Airlite Ti	LM/titanium	.32 H&R Magnum	1 7/8"/48 mm	6 cartridges	about 380 g	€ 1,012 (2003)
M 332 Airlite Ti Centenmal	LM/titanium, trigger DAO	.32 H&R Magnum	1 7/8"/48 mm	6 cartridges	about 340 g	€ 1,037 (2009)
M 337 Airlite Ti	LM/titanium	.38 Special	1 7/8"/48 mm	5 cartridges	about 340 g	€ 941 (2002)
M 337 Airlite Ti PD	LM (black anodized)/ titanium	.38 Special	1 7/8"/48 mm	5 cartridges	312 g	€ 1,041 (2004)
M 337 Airlite Ti Kit Gun	LM/titanium	.38 Special	3 1/5"/81 mm	5 cartridges	about 390 g	€ 883 (2007)
M 342 Airlite Ti Centenmal	LM/titanium, trigger DAO	.38 Special	1 7/8"/48 mm	5 cartridges	about 340 g	€ 1,034 (2003)
M 342 Airlite Ti Centenmal PD	LM (black anodized)/ titanium, trigger DAO	.38 Special	1 7/8"/48 mm	5 cartridges	about 340 g	€ 1,067 (2003)
M 36 LadySmith	Steel (blued)	.38 Special	1 7/8"/48 mm	5 cartridges	575 g	€ 693 (2007)
M-637 .38 Chief's Special Airweight	LM/steel	.38 Special	1 7/8"/48 mm	5 cartridges	about 420 g	€ 593 (2007)
M 638 Bodyguard Airweight	LM/steel	.38 Special	1 7/8"/48 mm	5 cartridges	about 425 g	€ 730 (2002)
M 638 Bodyguard Airweight	LM/steel	.38 Special	2"/51 mm	5 cartridges	about 430 g	€ 564 (2007)
M 642 Centennial Airweight	Alum/steel, trigger DAO	.38 Special	2"/51 mm	5 cartridges	about 430 g	€ 560 (2007)
M 640 Centennial Magnum	Stainless steel, trigger DAO	.357 Magnum/ .38 Special	2 1/8"/54 mm	5 cartridges	645 g	€ 635 (2007)
M 340 Airlite Ti SC Centenmal	LM/titanium, trigger DAO	.357 Magnum/ .38 Special	1 7/8"/48 mm	5 cartridges	about 340 g	€ 1,008 (2007)

M 360 Airlite Ti SC Kit Gun	LM/titanium (HiViz sights)	.357 Magnum/ .38 Special	3 1/8"/79 mm	5 cartridges	about 370 g	€ 1,109 (2003)
M 360 Airlite Ti SC Chief's Special	LM/titanium	.357 Magnum/ .38 Special	1 7/8"/48 mm	5 cartridges	about 340 g	€ 985 (2007)
M 60 Chief's Special Magnum	Stainless steel	.357 Magnum/ .38 Special	2 1/8"/54 mm	5 cartridges	about 640 g	€ 819 (2009)
M 60 Chief's Special Magnum	Stainless steel	.357 Magnum/ .38 Special	3"/76 mm	5 cartridges	685 g	€ 766 (2007)
M 60 Chief's Special Magnum	Stainless steel	.357 Magnum/ .38 Special	5"/127 mm	5 cartridges	864 g	€ 813 (2007)
M 60 Night Hunter	Stainless steel	.357 Magnum/ .38 Special	3"/76 mm	5 cartridges	about 680 g	€ 899 (2007)
M 649 Bodyguard Magnum	Stainless steel	.357 Magnum/ .38 Special	2 1/8"/54 mm	5 cartridges	640 g	€ 790 (2007)

* Manufacturer's information

J Frame Models, Technical Specifications and Prices

Manufacturer	Smith & Wesson Inc., Springfield, Massachusetts, USA				
Model	**M 337 Airlite Ti PD**	**M 36 Lady Smith**	**M 60 Chief's Special Mag**	**M 649 Body-guard Mag.**	**M 640 Centennial Mag**
Caliber	.38 Special	.38 Special	.357 Magnum/ .38 Special	.357 Magnum/ .38 Special	.357 Magnum/ .38 Special
Version	Alum. (black anodized)/ titanium	Steel (blued)	Stainless steel		
Weight	312 g	575 g	685 g	640 g	645 g
Cylinder capacity	5 cartridges				
Length	161 mm	161 mm	193 mm	172 mm	172 mm
Width	33.2 mm				
Height	110 mm	110 mm	132 mm	127 mm	127 mm
Trigger-backstrap distance	SA 61 mm DA 71 mm	SA 62 mm DA 72 mm	SA 66 mm DA 76 mm	SA 66 mm DA 76 mm	DAO 76 mm
Grip angle	110 degrees				

J Frame Models

Grip/grip panels	Combat	Fine wood	Combat		
Barrel	48 mm, five grooves right twist	48 mm, five grooves right twist	76 mm, five grooves, right twist	54 mm, five grooves, right twist	54 mm, five grooves, right twist
Cylinder diameter	33.2 mm				
Cylinder length	40.5 mm				
Cylinder gap	0.12 mm	0.15 mm	0.15 mm	0.30 mm	0.20mm
Trigger pull weight*	SA 13.39 N/1.37 kp DA 54.85 N 5.59 kp	SA 12.77 N/1.30 kp DA 53.65 N/5.47 kp	SA 13.09 N/1.34 kp DA 54.48 N/5.56 kp	SA 13.50 N/1.38 kp DA 53.78 N/5.49 kp	DAO 55.99 N/5.71 kp
Sight length/ line of sight over the barrel axis	93 mm/14 mm	90 mm/14 mm	124 mm/18 mm	96 mm/14 mm	100 mm/14 mm
Rear sight width/ front sight width	3.3 mm/3.3 mm				
Price incl. VAT	1,041 euros (2004)	693 euros (2007)	766 euros (2007)	790 euros (2007)	635 euros (2007)

*TriggerScan measurements

Trigger Pull Profile [N/mm]

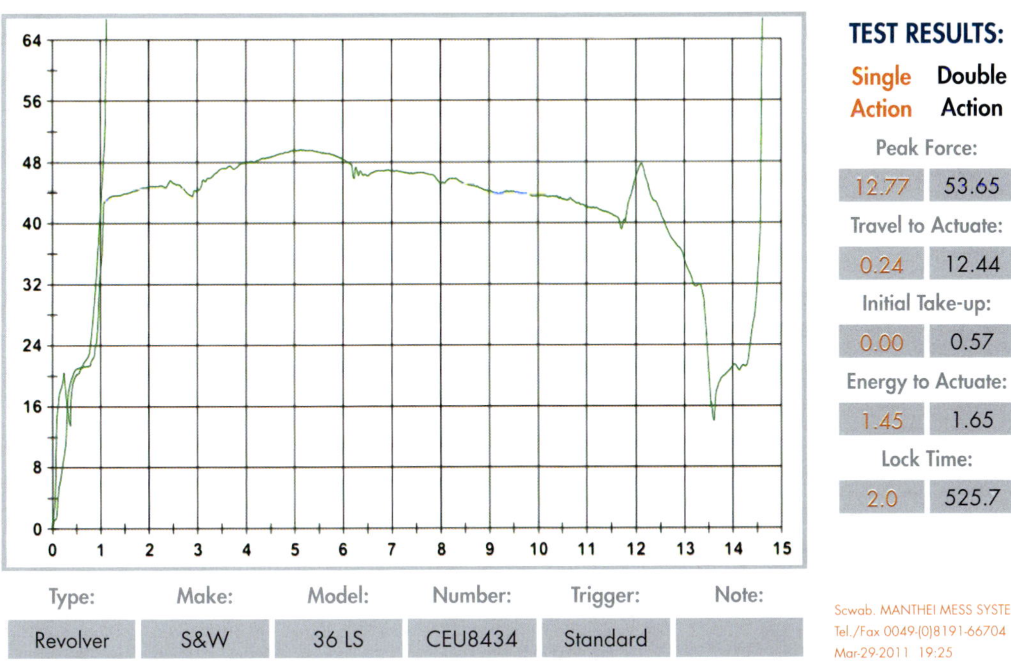

M 36 Lady Smith

Trigger Pull Profile [N/mm]

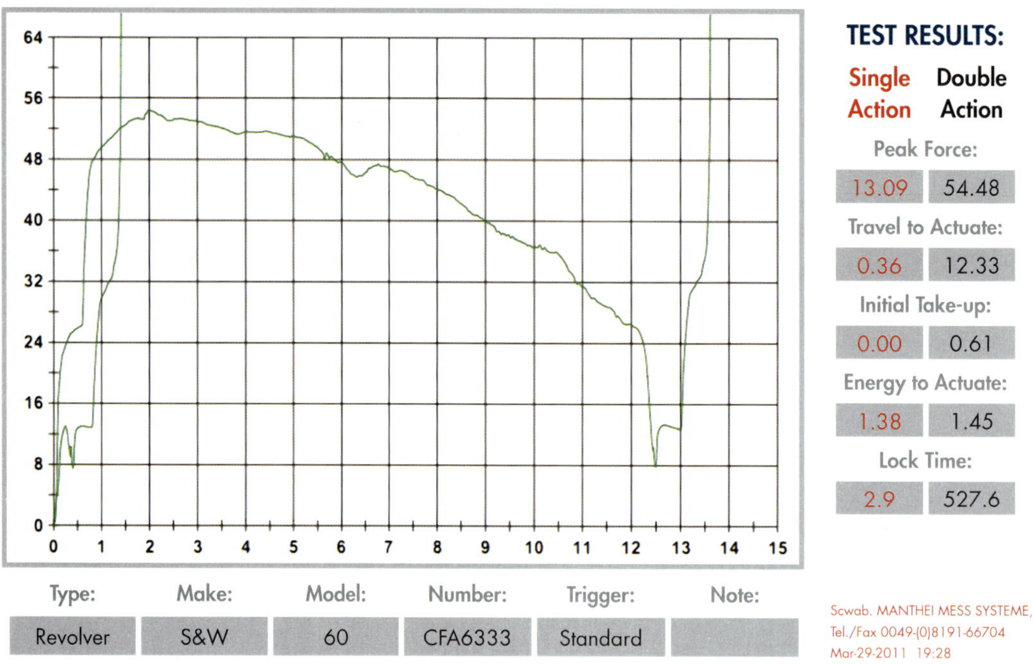

TEST RESULTS:

	Single Action	Double Action
Peak Force:	13.09	54.48
Travel to Actuate:	0.36	12.33
Initial Take-up:	0.00	0.61
Energy to Actuate:	1.38	1.45
Lock Time:	2.9	527.6

Type:	Make:	Model:	Number:	Trigger:	Note:
Revolver	S&W	60	CFA6333	Standard	

Scwab. MANTHEI MESS SYSTEME,
Tel./Fax 0049-(0)8191-66704
Mar-29-2011 19:28

M 60 Chiefs Special Magnum

Trigger Pull Profile [N/mm]

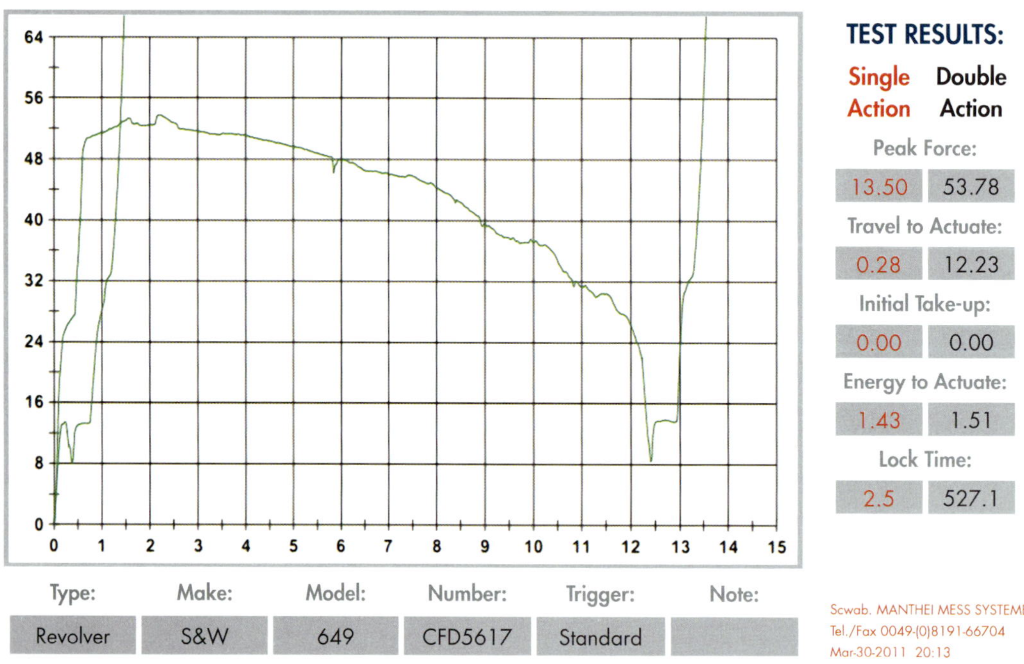

TEST RESULTS:

	Single Action	Double Action
Peak Force:	13.50	53.78
Travel to Actuate:	0.28	12.23
Initial Take-up:	0.00	0.00
Energy to Actuate:	1.43	1.51
Lock Time:	2.5	527.1

Type:	Make:	Model:	Number:	Trigger:	Note:
Revolver	S&W	649	CFD5617	Standard	

Scwab. MANTHEI MESS SYSTEME,
Tel./Fax 0049-(0)8191-66704
Mar-30-2011 20:13

M 649 Bodyguard Magnum

Trigger Pull Profile [N/mm]

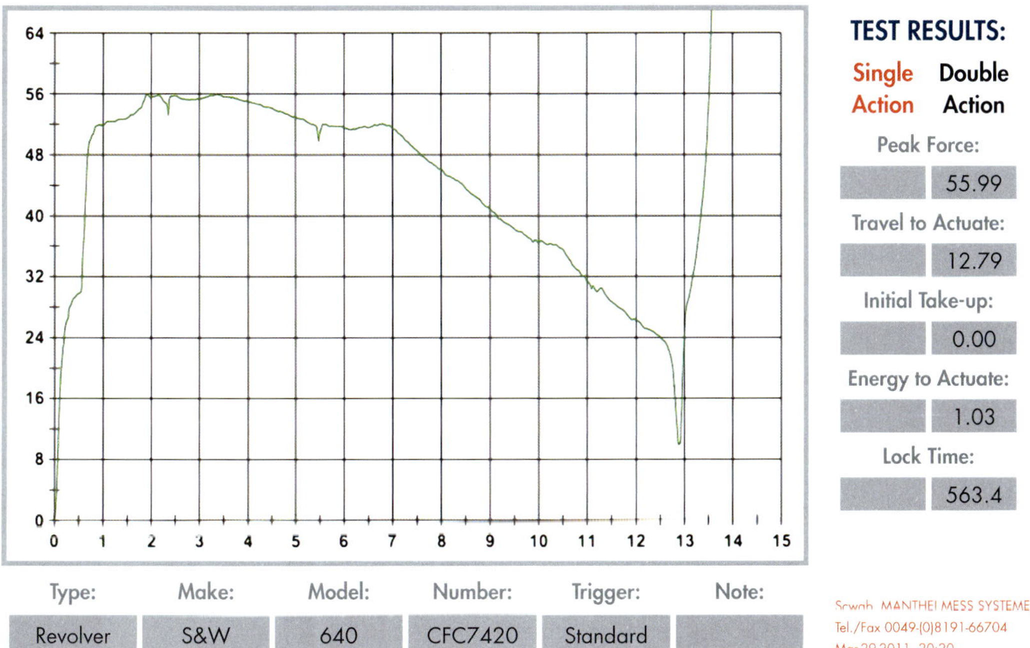

M 640 Centennial Magnum (DAO)

Korth

Weapons Manufacturer: Every Korth Combat, Sport, and Target Revolver Is Unique

So much elevated – and even over-the-top – praise has been written about Korth and "the" Korth, that here, it will be enough to indicate how Korth has fulfilled the highest quality standards and give a brief history of what ultimately became a very eventful. This small company – the number of employees at the time was five – was founded at a time when making and selling firearms was still prohibited, and private individuals could only shoot cartridge ammunition, pyrotechnic ammunition, irritants and other agents.

1954: Willi Korth makes his first gas revolver in the basement of his house in Ratzeburg. For the original and on-going series, he uses gun barrel steel from the Second World War; after the supplies were exhausted, he replaces this with other high quality steels. Quality is the paramount issue; this enables him to sell 20,000 pieces. The success also supports a move to a larger workshop.

1965: The era of precision Korth weapons begins. Willi Korth manufactures a small series of 300 service revolvers in .38 Special and, with the first civilian models of .22 l.r. to .357 Magnum, enjoys increasing popularity among shooters, hunters, and later also collectors. Despite the high prices, by 2002, Korth and his successors will sell over 18,000 service, combat, sports, and target revolvers, including limited anniversary editions, 300 stainless steel revolvers, 30 Triple Lock-type revolvers, 20 special Models, and also 280 pistols. By the end of 2002, serial number 39016 left Ratzeburg.

1981: Willi Korth sells his shares in the business to Alexander Kückens, Nicholas Graf von Bernstorff, and Uwe Dieter Kost. Korth GmbH & Co. KG is formed. Korth himself continues to work as production manager until 1983.

1989: Korth GmbH & Co. KG goes into financial settlement. A receiving company, the Korth Vertriebsgesellschaft mbH, under the management of Count von Bernstorff, takes over distribution of the stock and gets a manufacturing license the same year. The factory employs up to 30 people.

1999: Bankruptcy of Korth mbH.

2000: Gaston Freylinger, general manager of Armurerie Freylinger & Cie., a rifle manufacturer and weapons handler in Luxembourg, obtains the contract when Korth mbH is sold, and continues to operate the company as Korth Germany GmbH, with five employees from the old staff. Authorized representative Silke Musik, long-time sales manager for Korth, takes responsibility for the Freylinger daughter firm.

2001: Armurerie Freylinger & Cie. expands to the U.S. market. Korth USA founded in Tewksbury, Massachusetts.

2008: Closure of the factory in Ratzeburg.

2009: Korth Germany GmbH moves to Lollar, near Giessen. Andreas Weber becomes the new managing director.

Not all genuine authorized Korth revolvers are made according to the same design principle. The 1965 2 3/8 inch .38 still leans heavily on its American models, and an early six-inch .22 l.r. caliber Target revolver, .22 Winchester Magnum, and .357 Magnum only lock the cylinder in the breech face plate, unlock it by a latch on the left of the frame, and eliminated the need for an underlug. It is the Combat model which first combines everything that constitutes a Korth: tough, hard steel, excellent workmanship, and low tolerances, with superior ease of maintenance, reliability, and performance. Or in the copywriter's words: "Raw steel transformed into precision."

Up to 2003, the range included Combat, Sport, and target models in calibers .22 l.r., Winchester Magnum, .32 Smith & Wesson Long Wad Cutter, 9 mm Parabellum, 9x21 IMI, .38 Special and .357 Magnum/.38 Special, or, with

German workmanship: Korth. Some 70 percent of this Sport model is made of "man-hours," from the first milling operations on the forging blank of the frame, right up to the finishing touches. Standard features, interchangeable cylinder, and small parts, add up to 6,000 euros.

Sport Troy Model

Troy stands for the Trojan horse and touts the "Korth" in Korth: Without the gleaming surfaces, the Combat and Sport Trojans cost almost 25 percent less.

For special features, engravings and more, the sky's the limit where price is concerned. Already, deep-engraved arabesques decorating the plasma-coated surfaces cost 2,000 euros extra. And the golden dragon will only hiss for a five-figure euro amount.

an interchangeable cylinder, .22 Winchester Magnum/.22 l.r., .357 Magnum/.38 Special (only Combat), .357 Magnum/9x21 IMI, and .357 Magnum/9 mm Parabellum. Combat and Sport revolvers come in barrel lengths of 3, 4, 5 1/4, 6 and 8 inches; Target revolvers are available in 5 1/4 or 6 inches. The sights also vary: the Combat provides a rear sight set in the frame with elevation and windage adjustment, and a ramp front sight (Quickdraw front sight). The Sport model has a micrometer sight with fixed rear sight cutout and a hooked front sight; the Target revolver a micrometer sight with interchangeable rear sight blades and the same front sight. Rear and front sights are Korth products. There are also different grips, with smooth or checkered walnut, luxury grips of fine wood, and, hallmarked for the Target revolver, walnut grips with adjustable palm rest.

From 2004, in terms of mirror finish, the a few euros "poorer" Combat and Sport Troy models have featured a satin-blued finish. All other revolvers are mirror polish blued or given a plasma-surface coating (PVD) (plasma vapor deposition) with zirconium (anthracite), chromium-titanium (silver), titanium (gold), or titanium-aluminum (blue shimmer), and can optionally be made with almost any engraving. Prices range from 2,998 euros for the standard-version Combat and Sports Troy, to 5,585 euros for the plasma-coated Target revolver with interchangeable cylinder. Deep-engraved arabesques with platinum inlay on polished surfaces cost another 2,045 euros, and for the luxury revolvers with custom designs, monograms, emblems and the like, it is: Prices on request.

In terms of technology, there is no difference among the Korth newer models. Regardless of caliber and features, they still correspond to Willi Korth's first Combat, which already included the innovative, though not absolutely revolutionary, cylinder release using Korth's "little wheels" or rollers, to the right of the hammer; quick release of the cylinder crane; external fine adjustment of the trigger pull weight; and the double-action trigger with its versatile qualities. Only the material, and, in part, the manufacturing methods have changed. The frame, middle-sized by Smith & Wesson standards, emerges by sophisticated milling from a drop forged 16MnCr5 blank. Korth also uses the same high-strength chromium-manganese tool steel for the cylinder crane, the cylinder and barrel shroud. However, these parts are manufactured on CNC machines. In further operations, all surfaces receive their sharp-contoured cut, a case hardness of 56-61 Rockwell and – by time-consuming handiwork – their fine polishing.

Interchangeable system with quick-release lock: the touch of a button is enough to separate crane and cylinder from the frame. The conversion combination for shorter or longer cartridges snaps on the crane without any play, by using light pressure.

The frame, also very cleanly processed at the cutouts, carries the left-opening cylinder crane without noticeable play in a longitudinal bore, and locks the push button operated quick-change system of the crane lengthwise, also without play. The cylinder stop pressure pin turns on the crane axle; this sags after the crane/ cylinder unit is removed. The roller with the smallest axial and radial tolerances, rotates on the hollow shaft of the crane.

The six-shot cylinder used in all calibers displays finely turned chambers, a clearly defined smoke ring, and an exactly fitted ejector star with corresponding ID from the last digits of the serial number – in the pictured piece, 0-9-8-1 for 38981. In the caliber 9 mm Parabellum, a star with limited rotation replaces the external speed loader. Relatively strong springs in the underlugs and on the one-piece locking and ejector rod control contact on the breech face and resistance when the cylinder swings out and cartridge cases are ejected. The rod, which slides left when unlocking, moves over the cylinder hand slot.

The Korth's inner workings go on under the double screwed lock plate, left on the frame. A special notch in the opposite framee wall houses the spring-loaded release lever, which, by pressure on the "little wheel" or roller, turns around the

hammer pin and pushes the locking and ejector rod from the frame bores with the front of its triangle; it then pushes the form-fit head from a leftwards-opening bore in the underlug. The idea is to make it possible do everything with your right thumb and index finger, without changing the grip: the release and – which takes even more getting used to – swinging out the cylinder against the force of the strong locking spring. Under the release lever are the trigger cocking lever with the trigger spring. The regulating screw, which protrudes from the lock plate, serves as axle and counter bearing at the same time, and is secured to the right of the frame.

Experts and competitors alike consider the Korth trigger mechanism the ultimate revolver action. "There just isn't any alternative to this system," says one, who should know. Actually, to get a trigger mechanism like it, other manufacturers have to turn to already experienced gun tuners. There are seven basic parts, all manufactured to the highest precision standards and designed for minimal friction. The trigger is made in a modified tip-notch construction, so that the sharp-edged hammer tip and the cock notch direct the trigger. A slot in the front of the trigger controls the cylinder stop on float-mounted on the same axle – one of the polished lock plate screws – and spring-mounted in the crane axle.

Cylinder lock with cylindrical ejector rod tip in an exactly fitting lug bore …

… and the rod end in the breech face. This ejector star bears the ID 0-9-8-1, based on the revolver's number.

Opposite the hammer are the cock notch for single-action shooting and the cam, more or less needed for double action. This more or less depends on the diameter of the particular catch or pressure point wheel or roller being used. The trigger cocking lever is below the cam, and, beside the trigger, are the cylinder hand and hammer block, mounted in an L form around the pawl. The pressure point rollers and cylinder hand share a stud shaft, like the trigger cocking lever and hammer block. For the narrow grooved guide, a wider trigger shoe is available.

When ready to strike, the enclosed mainspring moves the hammer by the profiled head of its rod. The hammer turns left from the release lever around the common shaft, tapering before the pivot point to the wedge-shaped tip, bears the front side of the hammer lifter for double action, and, when the shot is released, drops on the spring-loaded firing pin in the frame. With its eleven millimeter wider spur, the Combat is also target grade. When the hammer is cocked, the mainspring, a long coil spring, can be set for "powerless" removal by a transverse bore in the case. The enclosed unit is again connected to hammer and square butt with the spring rod and a slot on the base of the case.

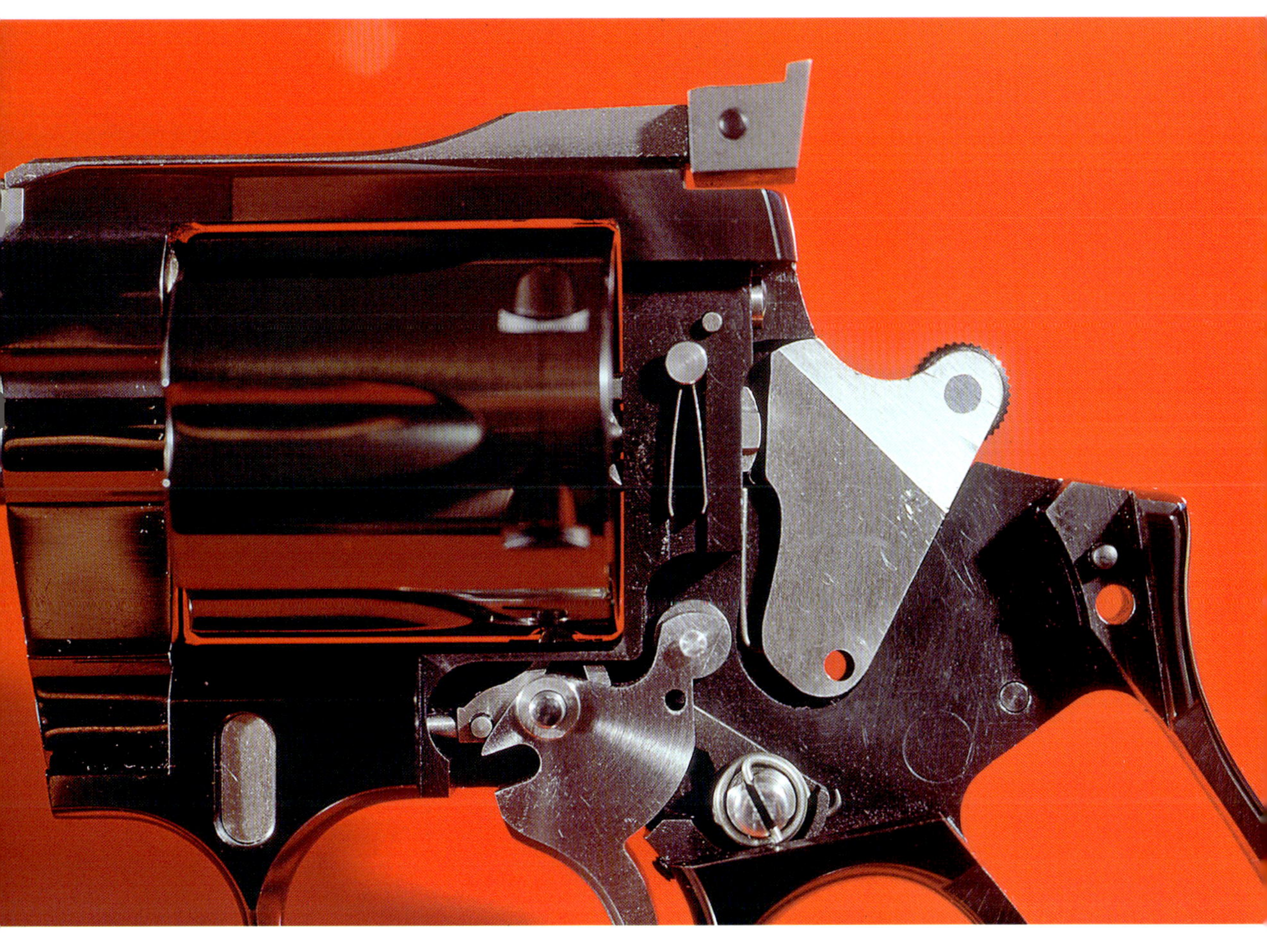

In single action, the trigger mechanism works in the conventional way. The tip or beak catches hold under the trigger until it clicks into the cock notch. Ultimately, the only resistance comes when getting out of the notch. When cocked, the trigger sits right in front of the trigger stop, a small hexagonal Allen screw in the trigger guard. While cocking the hammer, the trigger raises the cylinder hand on the ratchet of the ejector star, and rotates the cylinder to the next chamber. At the same time, it pushes the hammer block from the hammer travel path and pulls the cylinder stop from the right-turning cylinder until it clicks back into place. Finally, the profile on the mainspring rod releases the dropped hammer and guides it while the trigger and hammer block are again rest to the safety position. The externally adjustable trigger spring tension gives a wide leeway for setting the single-action trigger pull weight, without affecting the firepower of the system – for the Korth, between 10 to 20 Newtons. Under 11.42 Newton, however, 38981 quit its trigger return service.

Release lever with "Korth wheels" and push piece for the locking and ejector rod at rest.

Trigger mechanism technology at its finest: low-friction and adjustable. Behind the trigger, the spring with a slotted cocking bolt and cocking lever to readjust the trigger pull weight; below the trigger-linked cylinder hand and "redirected" hammer block, the pressure point roller, which is not visible in the reset position. This is used to adjust the double action trigger. The cylinder stop is about to be released.

Cocked: The hammer tip catches hold in the cock notch, the hammer block frees the hammer travel path, the pawl has rotated the cylinder by one chamber, and the pulled back trigger secures the engaged cylinder stop. In the middle of the picture, the now uncovered pressure point roller.

In double action, the trigger mechanism reveals its extraordinary capabilities. Korth's motto is "shooting with and without pressure points"; to make this possible, Korth provides three exchangeable small rollers, which have a big effect on force transmission from trigger to hammer. The three sizes – the minimal gradation indicates the level of precision in the whole system – guide the hammer lifter at different levels, up to the trigger or away barely above it, this way creating what Korth calls "variable pressure points." Roller 1 has a diameter of 7.2 millimeters and sets the spring-loaded catch hard enough to create a clearly identified pressure point of 29.8 Newton. Roller 2 measures 7.3 millimeters and transfers the hammer lifter, just touching. The trigger pull weight goes back to 27.3 Newton. And the 7.45 millimeter roller 3 brings the hammer to drop position without direct contact with the trigger. With this arrangement, the TriggerScan profile passes 17.5 Newton unimpeded. With its adjustment capabilities and a total resistance from cocking, rotation, and release, of only 38.94 (roller 1), 37.01 (roller 2) and 38.18 Newton (roller 3), this revolver is of shooting match quality.

Role playing: Depending on the size of the roller used, the revolver can be fired in double action at varying hardness, or without pressure point. With the small roller, the hammer lifter is set at hard. Using the middle roller, it only touches the cam. The large holds it at a distance until the hammer drops.

The profile on the mainspring rod guides the dropped hammer back to the reset position.

Not just for luxury models: rounded Menges barrel with eight grooves.

Sport Model

Both the classically beautiful wood grip panels and the barrel shroud contribute to the elegant appearance of the Korth revolver. Despite the underlug and barrel rib set on it, the very distinctive barrel shroud has a slim appearance. The "ventilation" of the longer rails (on four- to six-inch models) helps it at least appear to lose even more weight.

The uniform horizontal aspect fell victim to the same effect years ago. Since then, the defined barrel rib on the frame rises continuously to the pinned front sight, reducing any disturbing reflexes even better. In.22 l.r. caliber, the barrel shroud takes a cold-extrusion Lothar Walther barrel with six right-twist grooves and a twist length of 450 millimeters; the larger calibers have a rounded Menges barrel with eight right-twist grooves and a twist length of 400 millimeters. Depending on supply, Menges barrels are also available with six right-twist grooves and a twist length of 456 mm. All barrels are screwed into the frame and glued.

In 2003, the weapons magazine *Caliber* publicized another Sport model prototype as the "revolution from Ratzeburg": this features a four- and six-inch interchangeable system in calibers .357 Magnum and 9 mm Parabellum. The barrel can be changed using a spring-loaded stop in the barrel shroud, which can be pushed from a barrel latch near the muzzle and releases the now rotatable barrel for removal from the frame. Fine threads between barrel latch and the interchangeable barrels, allow for both barrel tension and cylinder gap within the system.

Korth Sport model/6 inch, Technical Specifications and Prices

Manufacturer	Korth Germany GmbH, Ratzeburg
Model	**Sport**
Caliber	.357 Magnum/.38 Special; optional Interchangeable cylinder .357 Magnum/9 mm Parabellum, .357 Magnum/9x21 IMI
Version	Steel, milled, smoothed, polished, blued. Fluted cylinder
Weight (with Sport grip)	1,150 g
Cylinder capacity	6 cartridges
Length	284 mm
Width (with Sport grip)	38.5 mm
Height	147 mm
Trigger-backstrap distance	SA 69 mm DA 78 mm
Grip angle	110 degrees
Grip	Sport, on request Combat, Target and Luxury. Special versions DSB, BDS, BDMR luxury models made from fine woods
Barrel	151 mm, eight grooves right twist
Cylinder diameter	38.5 mm
Cylinder length	41 mm
Cylinder gap	0.1 mm
Trigger pull weight *	SA 11.75 N/1.19 kp DA (roller 1/chamber 1) 38.94 N/3.97 kp (roller 2/chamber 1) 37.01 N/3.78 kp (roller 3/chamber 1) 38.18 N/3.89 kp SA adjustment range 10-20 N/1-2 kp
Sight length/line of sight over the barrel axis	200 mm/20 mm
Rear sight width/ Front sight width	3.5 mm/3.0 to 3.8 mm

Sport Model

Price incl. VAT (2004)	4,670 euros (blued), with interchangeable cylinder 4,962 euros (plasma coated matte/silver), with interchangeable cylinder 5,236 euros (plasma coated polished/silver), with interchangeable cylinder 5,356 euros (plasma coated polished/blue), with interchangeable cylinder Engravings from 2,045 euros Sport, Combat, Target and Luxury grips 118 to 260 euros Speedloader 24 euros
Prices incld. VAT (Standard versions 2007)	Combat Troy .22 l.r. 3-6 inches with interchangeable cylinder 5,120 euros Sports Troy .22 l.r., 4 – 6 inches with interchangeable cylinder 5,255 euros Combat Troy .357 Magnum, 3-6 inch 3,349 euros Combat .357 Magnum, 3-6 inch with interchangeable cylinder 5,120 euros Sport Troy .357 Magnum, 4-6 inch 3,349 euros Sport .357 Magnum, 4-6 inch with interchangeable cylinder 5,255 euros Target revolver .357 Magnum, 5 ¼ and 6 inch 3,679 euros Target revolver .357 Magnum, 5 ¼ and 6 inch with interchangeable cylinder 5,585 euros

*TriggerScan measurements

Trigger Pull Profile [N/mm]

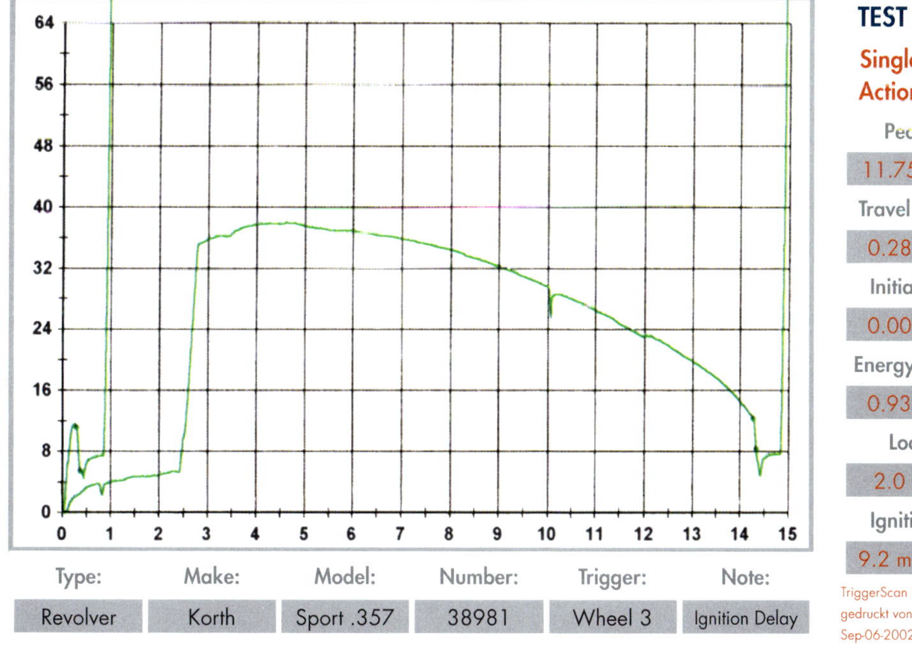

TEST RESULTS:

	Single Action	Double Action
Peak Force:	11.75	38.18
Travel to Actuate:	0.28	14.27
Initial Take-up:	0.00	0.12
Energy to Actuate:	0.93	1.29
Lock Time:	2.0	367.1
Ignition Delay:	9.2 ms	6.4 ms

TriggerScan 1,1, Nr. 10158,
gedruckt von Manthei-Mess-Systeme.
Sep-06-2002 17:21

Trigger Pull Profile [N/mm]

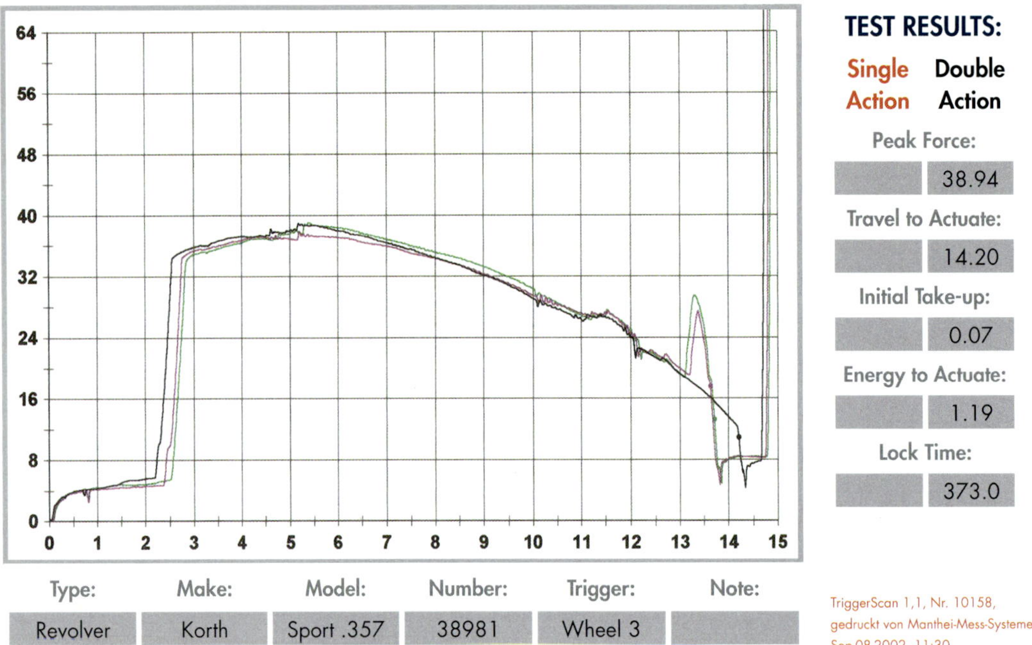

Changeable pressure point, with three exchangeable pressure point rollers (R 1, 2, 3) at 13.3 millimeters of double action travel to actuate.

Janz

It's a Bit Over, Okay? Large Calibers from Malente

What they really wanted was to continue making the Korth. Possibly also a Korth pistol. Uwe Janz, born in 1944, precision engineer and managing director of a family-owned company founded in 1935: JTL Janz Labortechnik GmbH, based in Malente, Schleswig-Holstein, Germany. And his 40-year professional colleague, Rene Ganz. In the late 1970s, Ganz was still training at Willi Korth, was promoted to workshop manager after getting his master's certificate. In 1997, under the pressure of the looming Korth bankruptcy, Ganz got this same position at JTL. Their joint wish is understandable: Already since 1994, Janz had been manufacturing precision parts for Korth on its modern machine tools, including cylinders, cylinder cranes, barrel shrouds and others; a desire to make a commitment to this manufacture that went beyond sub- contracting made sense. Ganz himself, in terms of all things "Korth," had a wealth of experience like no one else. However, those at Ratzeburg rejected the offer from Malente, and merged in 2000 with Armurerie Freylinger & Cie. in Luxembourg. Janz and Ganz took the rejection as a challenge. If not "the" Korth, then there should be another revolver in the high price range, an independent product that combined the tried and proven with new ideas; that is, a sort of Korth with even more potential applications. "As far as we were concerned," says Janz, "our idea was that there was no question of either a .357 Magnum limit to caliber, or any fixation on

The Janz represents consistent further development of the Korth revolver, with comparable level of quality standards, a caliber range from .22 l.r. to .500 Smith & Wesson Magnum, the option of hard caliber (E Series) or interchangeable systems up to .454 Casull (S series), barrel lengths ranging from 4 to 10 inches, and fully qualified to be in the high price range. The pictured S Class, as a .357 with fluted cylinder and short underlug, weighs just 1,495 grams, in accordance with DSB regulations.

The JTL shows its true colors featuring an unfluted cylinder and long barrel underlug. As a six-incher in .44 Magnum, it weighs 1,540 grams, as much as the Taurus Raging Bull.

hard caliber. Rather than compete with a new Korth owner on the old basis, we created a functional specification document, which initially provided for making a prototype .44, with interchangeable barrels and cylinders for all the usual calibers. The strongest caliber determined the size of the frame and the external dimensions of the cylinder. The wide range of Smith & Wesson-compatible grips recommended the round butt to us. For the interchangeable systems, we thought about a sight that always holds the center of the target, and as for the trigger mechanism, there is simply no alternative to Korth. We only needed to slightly change the geometry and fit it into larger frames. Everything else was the result of development." Janz and Ganz started operations in 1998, with a light metal frame as an object of study for CNC manufacturing.

1 V, the first prototype, with production number 001, successfully started firing shots in early 1999. In .44 Magnum caliber, this was the gun that launched the E series, augmented two years later with the S series, with interchangeable barrels and cylinders. But there was only limited joy about this successful piece. Janz wanted to make a revolver in an even larger and stronger caliber: .454 Casull. But that was just too much for the .44. So the team again bestirred the computer, recorded, programmed, changed mechanisms, and finally, that same year, presented their 2 V (No. 002) in .454 Casull. Eight other test pieces with different calibers, barrel lengths, sights, and other features followed, until March 2001, when, with number 010, actual mass production was launched.

To produce the S series' interchangeable barrels, JTL experimented first with defined barrel threading; the segments on the barrel and frame were designed to facilitate a quick change of caliber and barrel length by turning it 90 degrees when the pawl or hand is lifted, without have to use any tools. These so-called bayonet or gun catches soon gave way to a much simpler system, that has been mass produced since: The barrels are screwed into the frame by hand, with a M17.5 x l.75 trapezoid threading, secured there by the counter-rifling, and can be loosened again by hand. For hardship cases, every interchangeable system comes with plastic tongs, as an "orthopedic aid." A hardened and polished pin on the barrel shroud controls the impact on the frame side and catches hold outwards under the cylinder crane.

Starting production of the second series into was not under discussion for very long. About 90 percent of the buyers were already purchasing several calibers, in a surprise end-run around their authorized [German] firearms licenses, or upgraded later – what's the problem, if the main difference between a hard caliber and interchangeable system, is just a more or less tightly screwed barrel with a guaranteed force fit?

Just a small selection: interchangeable barrels, 4 to 10 inches. In terms of gas pressure, the KK cylinder gives basically no cause for concern.

After less successful attempts using gun-catch type thread segments, (1) Janz has relied on conventional threading. The screwed-in interchangeable barrels, which turn by hand to the stop position on the frame yoke …

Janz values independence. “Thanks to our CAD development and CNC manufacturing, we are able to manufacture all the revolver parts in-house, except the barrels and grips,” he says with pride, and at the same time refers to the flexibility this capacity provides. The rapid alterations made in the frames, and a later, just as spontaneous, weight reduction for the .357 Magnum system proves it. The frames are made by machining a three kilogram chromium-manganese steel block (16MnCr5) on the five-axis Deckel Maho in about three hours, yielding a “residual piece” of just 500 grams The tolerances? “Harrowing. It really means splitting hairs. The machine does its work to the thousandth part. Depending on the area, we are machining at between 0.01 and 0.001 millimeters.” For comparison: the average human hair measures 0.05 millimeters. Other parts still retain some excess material, such as the lock plate cutout, to allow for fitting work, grinding and polishing. Janz, incidentally, puts great emphasis on the fact that even when finished, the edges are still sharp and the rounded areas smooth. Cylinder crane and barrel shroud match the frame in material and workmanship while the cylinder, of a chromium-molybdenum steel alloy (42CrMo4), is manufactured on no less precise Fuchs automatic lathes. The selection of case hardened steels consistently of 60 Rockwell at 0.2 to 0.3 millimeters depth, is based primarily on their physical properties. A secondary issue is having the margins to get the same uniform hue if the material is to be blued.

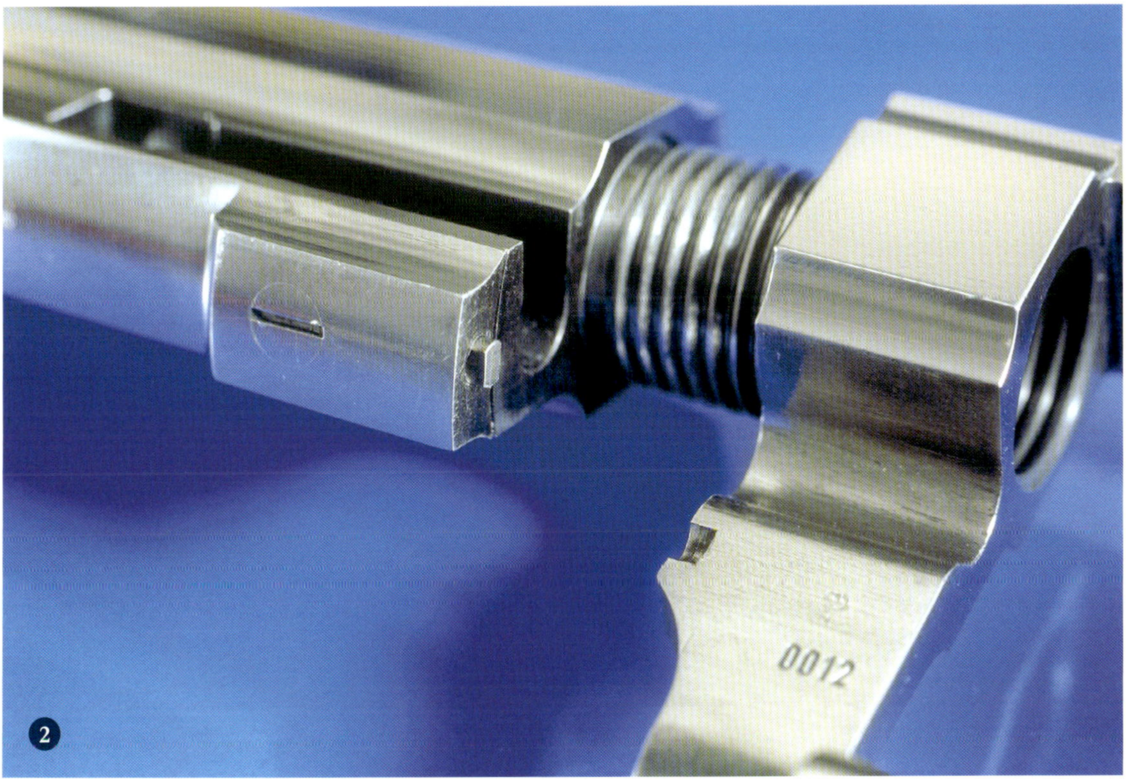

… (2) secure themselves by the counter-rifling, and lie on the crane …

… (3) under the breech.

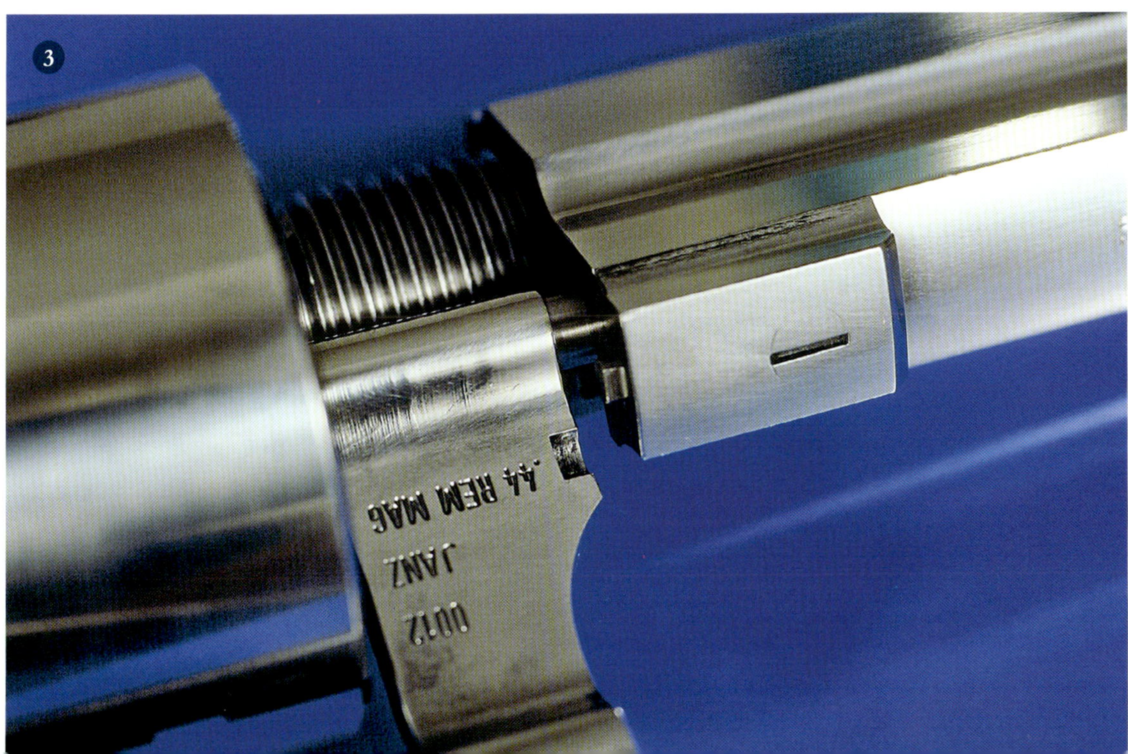

If you can't loosen the screws again by hand, the interchangeable barrel comes with plastic tongs as an "orthopaedic aid."

Three kilos of 16MnCr5, before and after machining.

No special discussion is necessary about the trigger mechanism. As in the Korth, it is mounted below a double screwed cover plate in the frame, is accessible from the left and uses almost carbon copy parts. Here again, the trigger is positioned on a milled lock plate screw and simultaneously controls the cylinder stop spring loaded on the crane axle, the cylinder hand, and the L-shaped hammer block. One of the selectively used pressure point rollers rotates opposite to the cylinder hand; in double action, the roller guides the spring loaded hammer catch at different heights, on the edge of the trigger or across it, thus creating or impeding a "rolling pressure point." In single action, the hammer tip engages out of range of the pressure point roller, in the cock notch of the trigger.

Other parts include the trigger cocking lever, adjustable from outside, the cylinder release lever, with its "goldilocks [little gold head]" instead of the black "Korth little wheel or roller," the enclosed mainspring and the mainspring rod, with a profile on its tip to release the dropped hammer and reset it. Ganz explains the relatively "serious" or "heavy" setting by the effect of the inevitable friction among mainspring, rod, and case on the impact impulse, which allows the smallest trigger pull weight for the series. Experimental best values lie at about 32 Newton.

At Smith & Wesson, the largest frames take only the largest cylinders. JTL has decided on another method, and, according to the caliber, makes from the uniform cylinder a five (.454 Casull), six (.44 Magnum, .45 Winchester Magnum and .45 Long Colt), seven (.38 Special and .357 Magnum) or eight capacity cylinder (.22 l.r.). But that's not always a good thing. What might benefit manufacturing, can also lead to not only a longer rotation-less bullet path, but also to weight where it hurts more. Thus, the revolver with the six-inch original system in .357 Magnum weighs just under 1,600 grams and could only be brought down to the DSB "fighting weight" of maximum 1,500 grams by abandoning a Janz feature, the unfluted cylinder, and other weight reductions – and this, compared to a Smith & Wesson, is still a decent weight.

The right rotating cylinder is mounted on the hollow shaft of the crane, and, like Korth, locks in the barrel shroud and on the breech face. A hard spring loaded catch bolt ensures that the cylinder stops, which pushes the locking and

Malente versus Ratzeburg: cylinder stop, trigger, cylinder hand, pressure point roller, hammer block, cylinder release, hammer, mainspring with rod and reset profile, housing, and trigger spring with cocking lever already in the frame – slightly modified and partially titanium treated.

ejector rods with its tip in a lengthwise bore in the barrel shroud and with the opposite end into the frame bores. There are other similarities, in the tight bearing tolerances, the surface quality of the fine-turned chambers, and a lower cylinder base in favor of a one millimeter high smoke ring. Also alike is the exact fitting of the cylinder star, the star's seamless operation of the pawl indents, and guidance of locking and ejector rods. When released, crane and cylinder swivel out to the left and, if desired, drop from the frame by pressing a button.

Whether for hunting, target shooting, or just for fun: the JTL revolver gets the full benefit out of its interchangeable systems. JTL offers eight barrel lengths in all calibers, between four and ten inches. For the smaller calibers, Janz prefers a Lothar Walther cold extrusion barrels with conventional groove and land profile; for the larger, cold hammered barrels of Peters steel with six segment polygonal rifling. "Of course, we also consider other barrel manufacturers, upon

Trigger with its "earmarked" cock notch, hammer with sharp edged tip and springloaded catch for the "rolling pressure point" in double action.

Uncocked trigger mechanism with engaged cylinder hand and hammer block in place.

Cocked trigger mechanism with rotated cylinder and hammer block pulled out of the way

Simplified trigger pull weight readjustment: Instead of double screwdriver for the spring tension bolt and attachment screw opposite, an Allen key is sufficient. A scale displays the lever position.

Trigger spring, spring tension bolt, and tension lever under the cocked hammer.

Free-ride effect: The smallest exchangeable roller sets the hammer lifter on the trigger, creating a clearly noticeable pressure point in double action. After the shot is fired, the springloaded catch swings through.

request, provided their products fit our concept" – this flexible businessman accommodates his customers, focusing especially on the essential right-twist rifling to safeguard the interchangeable barrels. In twist length, only the Lothar Walther .44 barrel, at 508 millimeters, differs from the other Lothar Walther (.22, .38, .357) and Peters steel barrels (.45, .454), which are uniformly drawn to 450 millimeters. All barrels include a forcing cone of eleven degrees, sit tight in the barrel shroud, and are pinned there almost like threading, to let the heat expansion of the screw connection drain off by the muzzle. Gradations of some 0.5 millimeters per caliber in the barrel outlet on the frame and barrel length, prevent a bullet accidentally hitting the wrong bore.

The requirement to keep the shot pattern constant, despite separating rear and front sights due to changes in caliber and barrel length, made it necessary for the manufacturer to develop their own sights. JTL first sought the solution in a backlash-free micrometer sight with elevation and windage adjustment with different height interchangeable front sights. This sighting arrangement, after careful zeroing in with the compatible front sights, faultlessly maintain the elevation, but not always the windage on longer barrels. The result was a new version, with windage adjustable only rear sight and elevation-adjustable front sight.

As the .454 Casull JTL already reveals: Only the currently largest caliber is strong enough for Janz and Ganz. And so the JTL 500 Premium in .500 Smith & Wesson Magnum tops its range – no lightweight, as a ten-incher, and, with this cartridge, no light fare for the shooter The .500 is based on the .44 frame, with expanded window for 15 millimeter longer cylinder, and is a descendant of the hard-caliber E Series with screwed and glued barrel. The latter is made by Lothar Walther, and has a right hand polygonal profile with eight segments and 406 mm twist. There were other alterations to the trigger, which only comes with a pressure point roller, the mainspring, the cylinder lock, and the sight.

Janz uses only its own sights. Here, an elevation and windage adjustable micrometer sight behind a non-elevation adjustable front sight. The interchangeable system can better maintain the shot pattern with a windage only adjustable sight behind an elevation adjustable front sight.

Janz JTL S- Series/6 inch, Technical Specifications and Prices

Manufacturer	JTL Janz-Labortechnik GmbH, since 2005, Janz-Präzisionstechnik GmbH, Malente, Germany
Model	**JTL S Series**
Caliber	Special Magnum/.38 .357 with interchangeable system .44 Magnum/.44 Special
Version	Steel, milled, smoothed, polished. Fluted or unfluted cylinder
Weight (with Sport grip)	1,495 g (.357), 1,540 g (.44)
Cylinder capacity	7 cartridges (.357), 6 cartridgess (.44)
Length	296 mm (.357), 295 mm (.44)
Width	45 mm
Height	147 mm
Trigger-backstrap distance	SA 84 mm DA 74 mm
Grip angle	110 degrees
Grip	Walnut, oiled
Barrel	153 mm, 6 grooves, right-twist, polygon (.357), 152 mm, 6 grooves, right twist, polygon (.44)
Cylinder diameter	45 mm
Cylinder length	46.5 mm (.357), 47 mm (.44)
Cylinder gap	0.1 mm (.357), 0.18 mm (.44)
Trigger pull weight *	SA 12.19 N/1.24 kp DA (wheel 1/chamber 1) 33.96 N/3.46 kp SA adjustment range 10-20 N/1-2 kp
Sight length/line of sight over the barrel axis	211 mm/22 mm
Rear sight width/ Front sight width	3.2 mm/3.5 mm

JTL

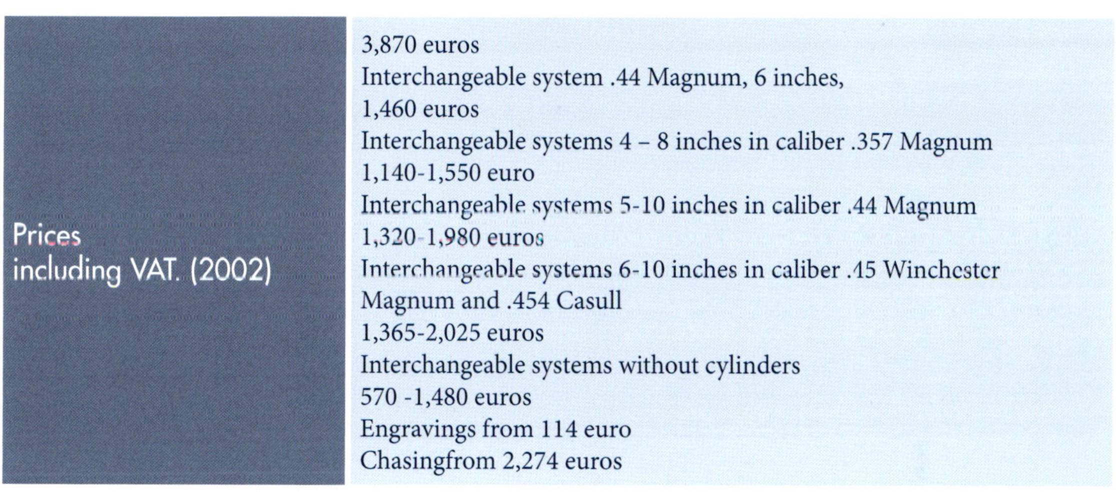

Prices including VAT. (2002)	3,870 euros Interchangeable system .44 Magnum, 6 inches, 1,460 euros Interchangeable systems 4 – 8 inches in caliber .357 Magnum 1,140-1,550 euro Interchangeable systems 5-10 inches in caliber .44 Magnum 1,320-1,980 euros Interchangeable systems 6-10 inches in caliber .45 Winchester Magnum and .454 Casull 1,365-2,025 euros Interchangeable systems without cylinders 570 -1,480 euros Engravings from 114 euro Chasingfrom 2,274 euros

*TriggerScan measurements

Trigger Pull Profile [N/mm]

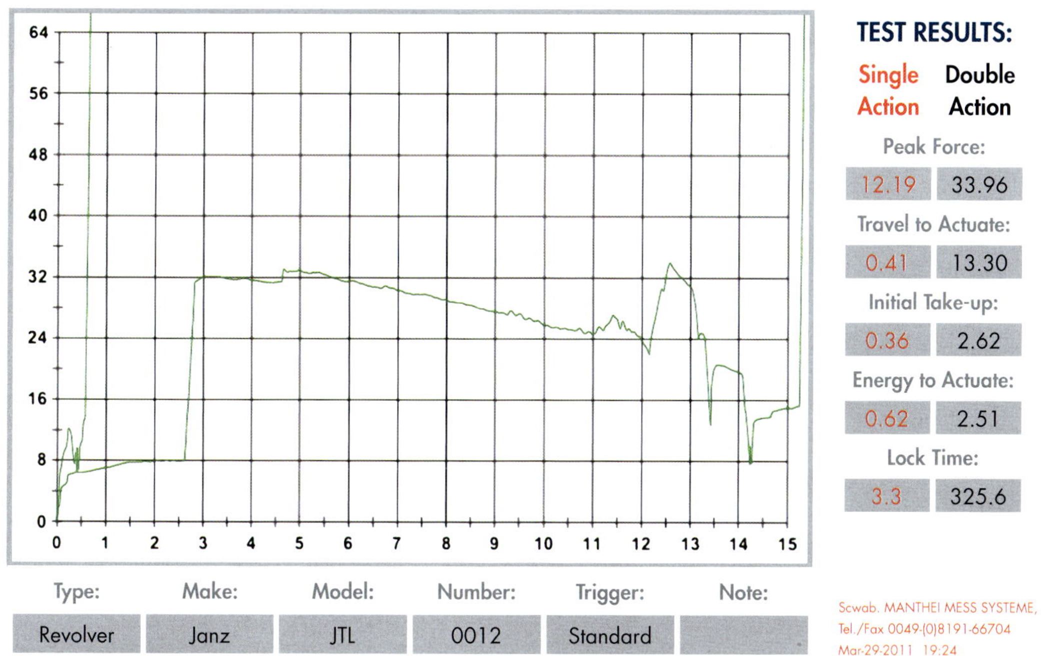

JTL, DA with smallest pressure point roller.

Weihrauch

A Good Offer from Bavaria: Magnums at a Discount

They should be inexpensive, reliable, and accurate: Weihrauch's Arminius triple-barrel Hunter, the uncompensated Target Trophy Combat with combat grip, and the compensated Target Trophy Match with match grip. All three are based on the proven 1976 HW 357. Nevertheless, these Bavarian revolvers are lower in demand with German shooters – apparently its maverick design is not so well received in this country, as the lines and technology of Smith & Wesson and Co., and it could also be that the moderate prices play a role which should not be underestimated.

At the end of the 1990s, Hermann Weihrauch Revolver GmbH, based in Mellrichstadt, Bavaria, Germany, took over revolver production and distribution from Hermann Weihrauch Sportwaffen KG, which had been based in the same location since 1948, The company manufactures a variety of models, centered on its target shooting flagship model HW 9 ST, a .22 caliber l.r. revolver with outstanding shooting performance. Weirauch makes a total of 43 double-action models in various versions, as well as three single-action models, which are offered in calibers .22 l.r. to .45 Colt with barrel lengths of 2 1/2 (HW 38/HW 357) to 10 3/4 inches (HW 9 ST/10 3/4), as firearms for hunting and snare-shooting, general purpose and target revolvers. There are also extra-long target versions and Western revolvers (WSA/Western Single Action). Prices range between 170 and 600 euros.

Whether the Arminius double action revolvers are made entirely of die-cast zinc or of steel with zinc die-casting, the frames are always two-part. Weirauch distinguishes these as the receiver or housing and grip piece. In contrast to

Heart shot: Axl (the dog) doesn't have to search it out and the lady hunter can really rely on her HW 357 Hunter. Fox terriers and three-inchers are ideal hunting companions.

Optimum cost/benefit ratio: For only 536 euros, the uncompensated HW 357 Target Trophy Combat can offer plenty of bull's eyes. With a 25-meter target, as from the Korth-Janz faction, the large caliber Arminius can almost compete with the small caliber HW 9 ST.

one-piece frame design, in the Weirauch, receivers and grip pieces have strictly separate functions: parts of the trigger mechanism take action only from from the grip piece. The Hunter and Target models are made in this hybrid design, with hardened precision casting for the upper part and NE (non-ferrous) alloy for the lower.

Upper and lower parts are inserted one into the other, with the sides of the 18 millimeter wide receiver overlapping the some eight millimeter narrower grip section. Alignment pins on the trigger guard and coaxial in the hammer bushing secure the lower part. The receiver or housing contains the barrel threading, crane bearing, double cylinder lock, firing pin with spring, impact ring and nut, and the cutouts for cylinder stop and cylinder hand, and the cylinder release slide and cross-pinned adjustable sight on the bridge. Not all details are based on the usual standards. The barrel protrudes only a few tenths of a millimeter into the cylinder

window, to prevent possible cracking from heat expansion in the forcing cone. Under the bridge, a curve in the swing direction compensates for the narrow distance of the receiver from the cylinder. Instead of a crane in the half-profile of the frame yoke, an integrated swivel arm folds out of the receiver. A segmented ring on the yoke and swivel arm takes over forward cylinder locking. When the cylinder is swiveled in, the ring closes around a sliding breech case. The system for the back lock – locking spindle (locking and ejector rod) in the breech face – is less original. To unlock, the release slide pushes the locking spindle over indent and bolt, and at the same time, the breech case from the breech face and the front lock, releasing the cylinder, which swings out leftwards for reloading. However, the only 17 millimeter rod and the 39 millimeter short cylinder hinders the shooter when reloading, as does the quite experimental reloader.

The impression is deceptive: Under the barrel shroud with integrated compensator, the HW 357 Target Trophy Match's barrel is only 121.5 millimeters long. The high-level impact safety reduces possible sports applications, according to the usual rules.

This family photo doesn't necessarily show that barrel and grip assembly make almost all the difference.

Like the receiver, cylinder and accessories, the grip piece, grip, and trigger mechanism are a solid unit, which can be removed as a complete piece from the receiver through the hammer bushing (hammer pin), thanks to the ingenious pinned fitting between the parts. The trigger system is designed as a conventional reset trigger mechanism, with an automatic hammer block firing pin safety. Depending on whether you fire the gun using single or double action, hammer or trigger activate either the cock notch or free drop, by disengaging the hammer

strut. As the revolver is cocked, the trigger lifts the left-linked cylinder hand into the cylinder star ratchet, tips the spring loaded cylinder stop lever from the rotating cylinder, and pulls the right linked hammer block out of the hammer travel path. A coil spring in the backstrap generates the impact energy. After the shot is fired, the released trigger guides the hammer over an intermediary lever back to reset position. Specifically for target shooting, the Target models include another adjusting screw, well covered from the grip, to regulate the trigger pull weight, and an adjustable trigger stop on the trigger guard. Both Hunter and Target models have a wide trigger shoe.

The Hunter goes hunting, three inches long. Its 76-millimeter barrel features six right-twist grooves with a twist length of 476 millimeters; it also gives a thoroughly attractive shooting performance at 25 meters, although that is not so relevant for hunting. After all, getting a 35 millimeter group using adjustable target sights justifies an occasional infidelity into practicing target shooting. Like the underlug, the front sight saddle and ramp front sight are part of the barrel shroud, which is screwed and pinned into the barrel near the muzzle. A handy Combat grip rounds out the general features.

Weirauch divides his revolver frames into receiver or housing and grip piece; these are manufactured either both in die-cast zinc, or from steel and non-ferrous alloys. In the .357 range, the steel housing takes the barrel and cylinder crane; the complete trigger mechanism and mainspring are in the non-ferrous grip piece.

Dowel pins in the hammer bushing and trigger guard fasten the grip piece into the receiver.

Target Trophy Combat and Target Trophy Match have different barrel length, and also more or less different active inner workings in the equally long barrel shrouds. In the uncompensated modes, barrel and shroud lock with the muzzle, while the compensated version barrel, which is 24.5 millimeters shorter, still has room in the barrel shroud for an expansion chamber with eight ports. Both barrels feature the same profile as the three-inch model, and both barrels carry a grooved rib for the sights running up to the front target sight, four threaded bores for attaching optional visual or electronic sights, and the distinctive triple screw connection on the barrel. The somewhat clumsy rear sight has a backlash-free precision catch for the windage adjustment screw and provides a high-contrast line of sight at the same gap width behind the 3.5-millimeter front sight.

The barrel locks by the spring loaded locking spindle in frame yoke and breech face. A segmental ring on the yoke and crane locks the front. When the cylinder is swung out, it locks the spindle on the breech case …

… to unlock, the pushed-forward case releases the spindle.

The 17 millimeter rod is little more than half the length of the breech case.

Weihrauch HW 357 Hunter/3 inch and Target Models, Technical Specifications and Prices

Manufacturer	Hermann Weihrauch Revolver GmbH, Mellrichstadt, Germany		
Model	**HW 357 Hunter**	**HW 357 Target Trophy Combat**	**HW 357 Target Trophy Match**
Caliber	.357 Magnum/.38 Special		
Version	Steel/zinc die cast, blued. Fluted cylinder		
Weight	870 g	1,090 g	1,185 g
Cylinder capacity	6 cartridges		
Length	193 mm	271 mm	298 mm
Width	37.5 mm	37.5 mm	52.5 mm
Height	143 mm	152 mm	152 mm
Trigger-backstrap distance	SA 62 mm DA 71 mm	SA 69 mm DA 72 mm	SA 70 mm DA 79 mm
Grip angle	120 degrees		
Grip/grip panels	Combat (wood), one-piece	Combat	Adjustable Nill grip
Barrel	76 mm, six grooves right twist	146 mm, six grooves, right twist, uncompensated	121.5 mm, six grooves, right twist, compensated
Cylinder diameter	37.5 mm		
Cylinder length	39 mm		
Cylinder gap	0.3 mm	0.15 mm	0.2 mm
Trigger pull weight*	SA 22.81 N/2.33 kp DA 58.21 N/5.94 kp	SA 20.33 N/2.07 kp DA 64.15 N/6.54 kp SA adjustment range from about 14 N/1.43 kp	SA 15.29 N/1.56 kp DA 51.09 N/5.21kp SA adjustment range from about 14 N/1.43 kp
Sight length/ line of sight over the barrel axis	124 mm/22 mm	193 mm/20 mm	193 mm/20 mm
Rear sight width/ front sight width	2.5 mm/3.0 mm	3.5 mm/3.5 mm	3.5 mm/3.5 mm
Price incl. VAT	298 euros (2010)	536 euros (2010)	505 euros (2010)

*TriggerScan measurements

HW 357

Trigger Pull Profile [N/mm]

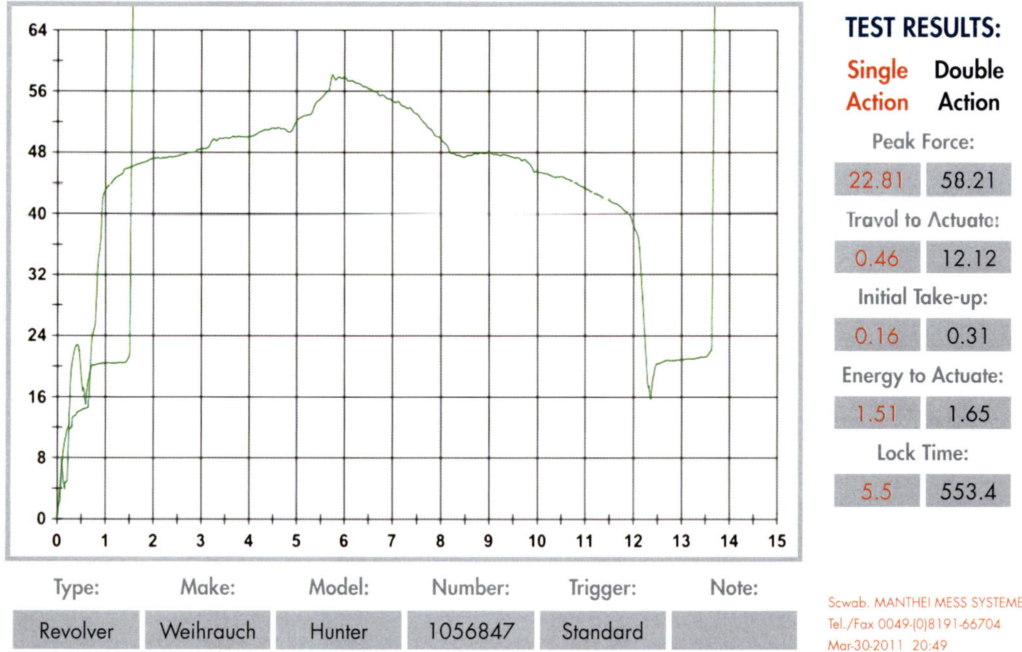

HW 357 Hunter

Trigger Pull Profile [N/mm]

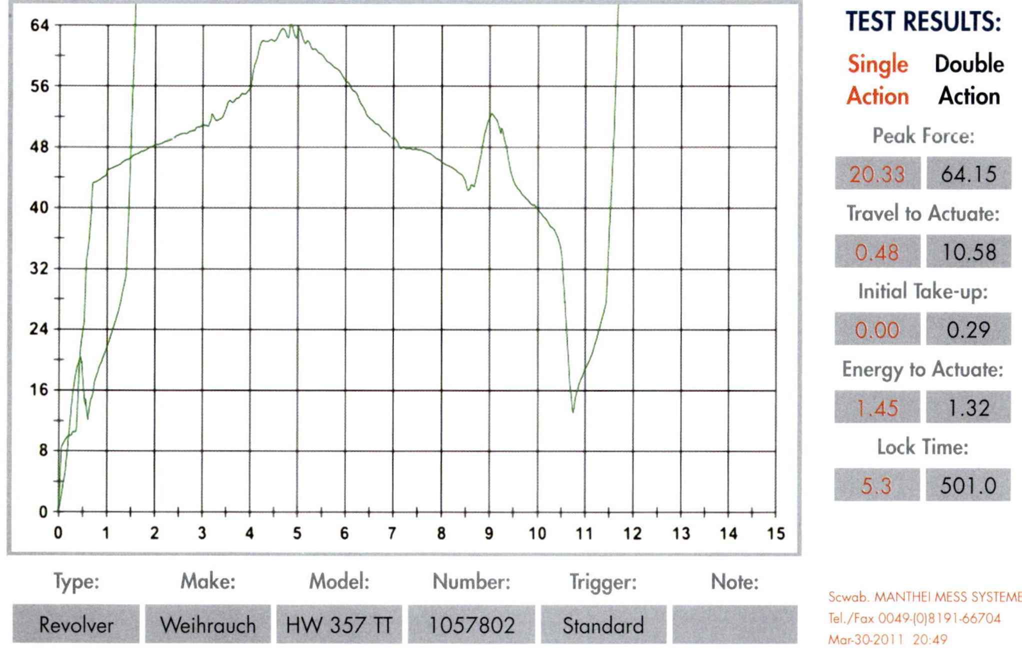

HW 357 Target Trophy Combat

Trigger Pull Profile [N/mm]

TEST RESULTS:

	Single Action	Double Action
Peak Force:	15.29	51.09
Travel to Actuate:	0.34	11.46
Initial Take-up:	0.00	0.25
Energy to Actuate:	0.77	1.42
Lock Time:	3.5	461.6

Type:	Make:	Model:	Number:	Trigger:	Note:
Revolver	Weihrauch	HW 357 TT	1057801	Standard	

Scwab. MANTHEI MESS SYSTEME,
Tel./Fax 0049-(0)8191-66704
Mar-30-2011 20:48

HW 357 Target Trophy Match

Sturm-Ruger

Investment-Cast Revolvers

In 1948, more than half a century after Colt's innovative advance created the first functioning swing-out cylinder revolver with double action trigger (Navy Model 1889), businessman Alexander McCormick Sturm and weapons expert William Batterman Ruger founded Sturm, Ruger & Company Inc. in Southport, Connecticut. These newcomers, instead of taking on the general trend in revolver development, at first started supplying the market demand for single action revolvers, which had been woefully neglected by their competition. With their small- and large-caliber Single Six and Blackhawk revolvers, Sturm, Ruger did as good a business as it had with its earlier small caliber Standard pistol had done, even after Sturm's early death in 1951. Ruger continued to run the company under its familiar name and – true to the company motto: "Always the right product at the right time" – only got serious about double action revolvers towards the end of the 1960s. The Security Six, Speed Six, and Police Service Six came on the market in 1971.

Sturm, Ruger continued to modify the .357. In 1973, they furnished them, as new models, with a transfer bar safety, and in 1979 finally saw that the time had come for a .44 with double action trigger. The expanding company continued its successful sales with these developments, although that success at one time had been based on Colt's development in the opposite direction – Smith & Wesson also, at times. The other basis for Sturm, Ruger's success was the favorable ratio of price to performance of its products, due to its efficient production methods. Already by 1949, Sturm, Ruger was making the Standard from pressed steel parts with welded joints, while the established brands were still milling their small caliber pistols from blocks. In the following period, Sturm, Ruger perfected use of investment casting techniques to make frames, accessories and trigger pieces of the other weapons. As a specialist in lost-wax investment casting, the company has enjoyed worldwide acclaim in the industry ever since.

Redhawk

Sturm, Ruger makes the Redhawk in .41 Magnum, .44 Magnum and .45 Colt calibers as an appropriately solid piece. Despite the relatively modest 5 1/2 inch barrel length and short ejector rod housing or underlug, the Redhawk has a considerable empty weight of 1,375 grams, due to large material reserves on the frame and cylinder – the bridge cross section alone measures 18 x 7 mm. For its "mechanical characteristics," the Instruction Manual lists double cylinder locking directly in the frame, universal use of an ejector rod that does not rotate with the cylinder, a central spring for both trigger and hammer together, the transfer bar safety, and the capability for removing trigger mechanism and cylinder without using any tools. An easily activated pin just to fix the pre-tensioned trigger- and mainspring on the guide rod is hidden by the grip panels.

The solid investment cast frame is distinguished not only by its ample dimensions at the more stressed points. The supporting structure is made even more stable, by omitting the large side plate to accommodate the trigger mechanism and adjacent parts. Based on the proven design of the single-action revolver, the Redhawk frame trigger guard, crane lock, trigger, cylinder stop, cylinder pawl, and transfer bar are inserted modularly. The one-piece frame ends in a square butt, which can be seen between the wood grip panels.

With the requirement that the force be absorbed at the most "congested" points, Sturm, Ruger developed a slightly different cylinder lock. While Colt revolvers lock only in the breech faceplate, and Smith & Wessons on both sides by the combined locking and ejector rod, in the Redhawk, the cylinder crane is fixed in the frame yoke and it uses a rod that engages in the breech face as the primary mechanism to lock and unlock the whole system. The locking rod, which swings in with the cylinder, is deflected by pressure from the beveled breech plate on the ejector star, and is temporarily levered by the front end of the crane latch away from the crane rotation. On impact, both parts rebound and click into place at the same time in the corresponding frame cutouts. Due to the quality of the locking system and the careful distancing of the crane stop, there is minimal side-play, hardly noticeable when the hammer is cocked. To unlock, a convenient push button replaces the link in the frame; in its turn, the button shifts the locking bar along with the bolt, until they come out of the frame together.

The Ruger Redhawk is distinctly different from the other representatives of the .44 Magnum class, not only in its high precision investment casting, generous dimensions and greater stability, due to its solid frame on both sides. It also has a trigger mechanism, cylinder lock, and an ejector rod that doesn't rotate with the cylinder ejector rod; features which don't exist in other systems.

The Redhawk's special attraction is unquestionably its nostalgic appeal, a tribute to the Single Six and Blackhawk revolver from the early days.

In the Redhawk, the main spring functions with both trigger and hammer at the same time, via the trigger bar and the tension lever linked to the frame.

When the gun is cocked, the mainspring can be fixed with an attached pin through the transverse bore of the trigger bar.

When the gun is uncocked, the fixed spring releases the tension lever, which then can be lifted from the bearing and hammer stirrup and used as an extra tool for removing the trigger unit.

The six-shot cylinder, mounted conventionally on the crane hollow shaft; swings out leftwards as required; it also rotates to the left, so that the spring loaded locking bolt will not travel over the pawl slot every time the revolver is reloaded, as reloading, in the way of designs less sparing of material. The cylinder, already a generously sized CNC lathe part, is reinforced further by locking grooves which are offset due to the asymmetric setting of lever and chamber bores; in this critical area also, the bores are at least three millimeters from the outer wall.

To ensure the right dimensions from frame and barrel to the high swing range of the bolted crane per caliber, the ejector rod is lowered slightly in relation to the cylinder pin. In addition, the lock's space requirements and operating it by the locking rod, makes it necessary to have a slotted ejector rod; this slides over the lock lever arm and the higher-set ejector against the force of the shared spring, to eject the cartridge cases. Since the ejector rod neither aligns with the lock bolt nor rotates with the cylinder, the two parts are only loosely interconnected by the rounded screw head of the spring retainer in the ejector. The star-shaped ejector is molded integrally with the pawl teeth and is secured against rotation by its profiled hub and two alignment pins in the cylinder base.

Only hammer, spring tension lever and recoil spring are mounted in the frame. All other parts of the mechanism are components of the trigger module: Trigger, trigger bar with main spring, cylinder stop, cylinder pawl and hammer strut.

The cylinder stop, trigger tip and cocking lever, hammer strut and cylinder pawl project from the precision-fit trigger guard breech.

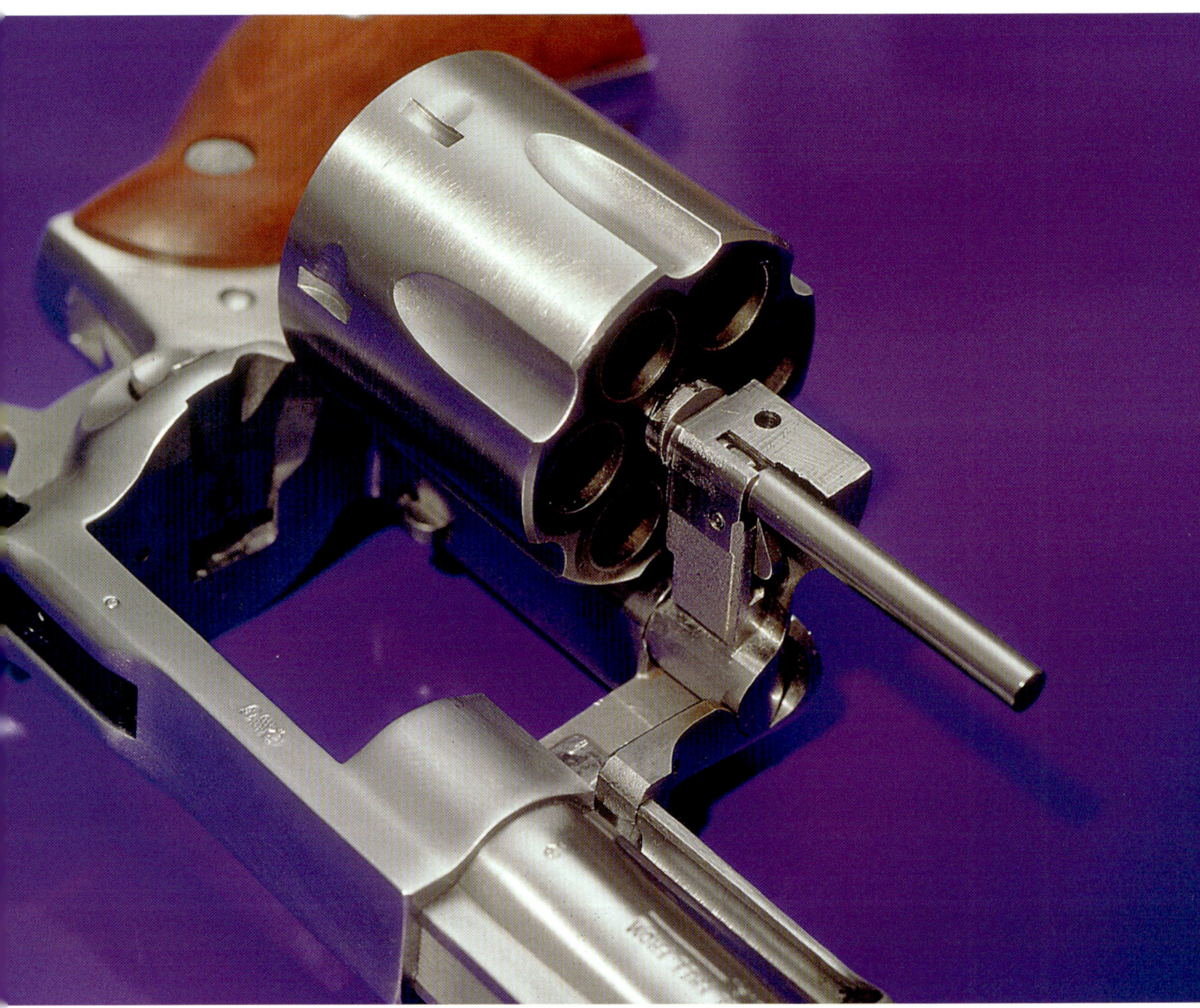

A pivot bolt on the crane replaces the traditional cylinder lock. Movements into and out of the frame yoke are subject to positive control by the locking bar. When the cylinder is swung in, it engages with the breech face and brings forward the lock at the same time. Pushing the release lever on the cylinder shield does the opposite.

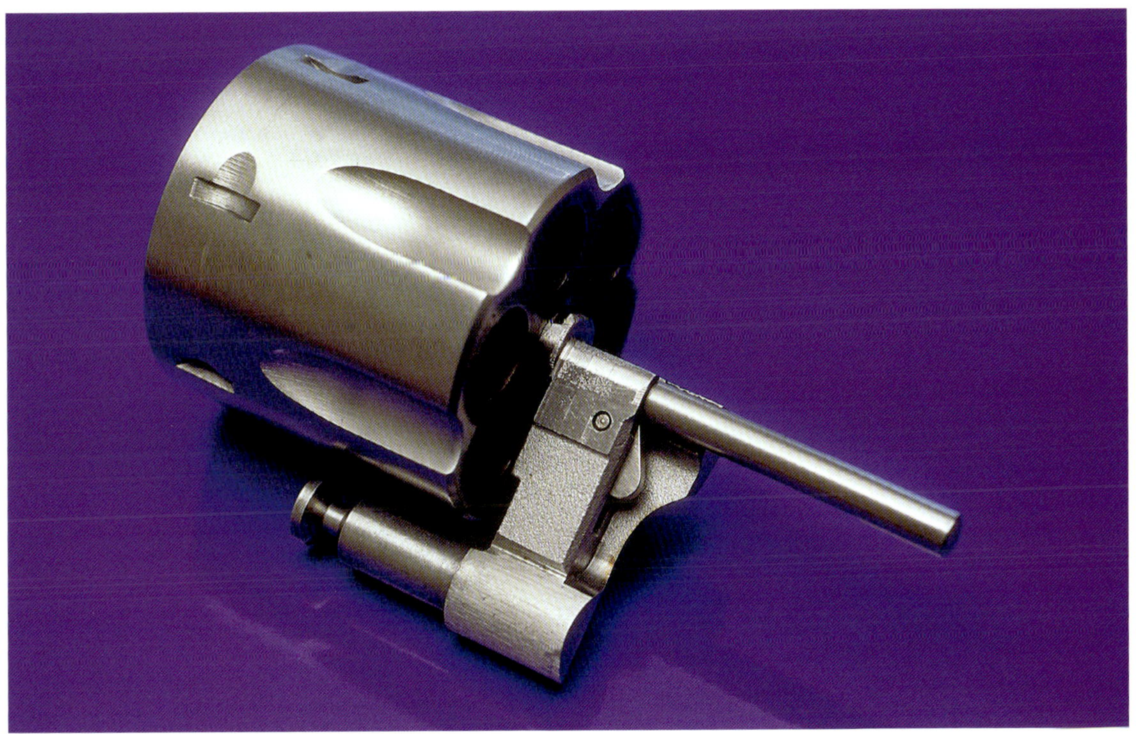

By lowering the ejector rod in relation to the cylinder pin, the crane loses design height. The "misalignment" between ejector and locking rods is compensated by the rounded screw head of the spring retainer.

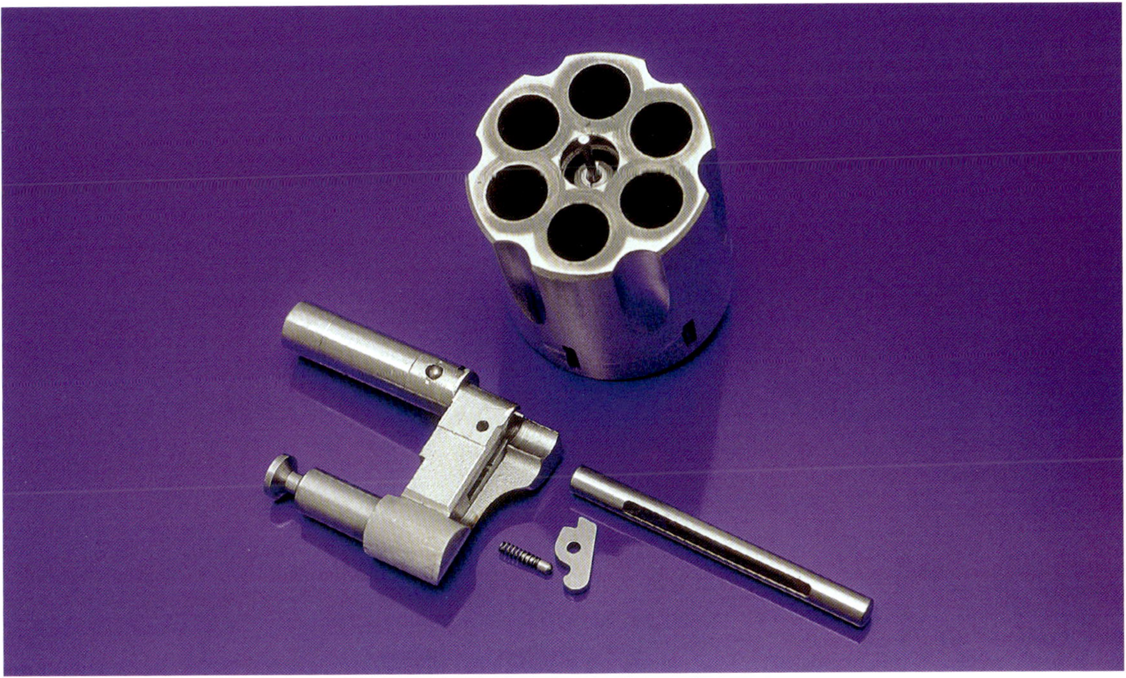

The slotted ejector rod overtops the swivel bolt and moves the ejector by the spring retainer easily visible in the cylinder and locking bar.

The side-opening frame guides the crane bearing mostly independently of other functions. In the Redhawk design, which opens underneath, the crane bearing latch is covered by the trigger unit, and can release the crane only after the removal of the trigger and mainspring modules, the hammer and the remaining parts of the trigger mechanism. Thus only the grip requires a screwdriver – the case rim recommended by optimists will never reach the deep-set screw slot. The rest can be done using the supplied spring tightening pin, with the spring tension lever raised out of the hammer stirrup as an auxiliary tool for unlocking the trigger unit, and a bit of manual dexterity. Especially noteworthy are the simple fixing of the hammer pin in the frame through the right grip panel, and the precisely fitted workmanship of the frame and trigger mechanism contact surfaces

Compared to conventional designs with slanted mainspring and additional trigger spring, the Redhawk trigger mechanism central spring is horizontal in the frame and compressed in the opposite direction by the trigger bar and the frame-supported tension lever. In single action, the hammer engages with the sear under the trigger tip, turns the trigger against the proportionate force of the coil spring until it clicks into place backwards, and makes its own show of strength as the tension lever is drawn. The force distribution results from the leverage ratios. In double action, the trigger engages under the moveable hammer catch, switches to the fixed cocking lever, and finally positions the hammer ready to drop. To rotate the cylinder to the left, the trigger mechanism uses a lever, "outsourced" far to the right like the cylinder stop. From the left, the trigger guides the Iver Johnson-inspired transfer bar alternately into the safety or firing position. Most of the fixed and all moving parts of the trigger system are cast, peened or polished and smoothed to the right size at the relevant points. However, the hammer-cocked trigger mechanism conveys the sensation that the trigger and hammer are being adjusted before moving out of the notch. The timing positions the rotated chambers forward to the hammer, behind the barrel.

At an empty weight of some 1,400 g, a 5 1/2-inch barrel with a shorter ejector rod housing was in order – for long-range shooters, a 7 1/2-inch model is also available. The 140-millimeter barrel features six right-twist grooves in the groove/land ratio of 10.9/10.6 millimeters, a 5.2-millimeter 11 degree forcing cone, a 3.1 millimeter wall at the barrel entrance and a deep-recessed muzzle. This thick-walled tube carries an equally robust sight rib, which accommodates a 3.5 millimeter wide interchangeable ramp front sight with orange plastic insert; an adjustable white 3.5-millimeter rear sight is set on the frame bridge.

Super Redhawk

The Super Redhawk is already in the next weight and performance class. Revolvers over 1,500 grams and with 6 1/2 inch barrels are not the subject of this book. However, for comparison – and also to eliminate any confusion – we will at least describe here the "Super's" main differences from its namesake. The frame of this 1987 model, for internal fittings and for the GP-100 recoil-reducing grip, was given a rack the length of the short underlug, to better control barrel oscillations, to make it possible "to get a better grip on" the barrel with the 62 millimeter long threading, and to provide a telescopic sight mount. With six shots, the fluted or unfluted barrels, depending on caliber, maintain the three-millimeter safety distance of the chamber bores from the exterior, and the 7 1/2 and 9 1/2 inch barrels in caliber .44 Magnum, .454 Casull and .480 Ruger manage the decreasing external diameters close to the muzzle without sight rails.

Series GP-100

Probably under the influence of the new Smith & Wesson L frame models 586/686 Distinguished Combat Magnum (1981), Sturm, Ruger also modernized their middle-sized class. The 1985 four- to six-inch GP-100, as the successor to the former .357, combines the good features of the Security Six series with the basic concept of the Redhawk and meanwhile found itself, like the competition, in a whole new model range – of course with investment casting of blued chrome molybdenum steel or rust-resistant chromium-nickel steel. The primary resemblance to its forebears include the separation of frame and trigger unit, firing pin safety by the transfer bar, and the cylinder lock specifically taken over from the Redhawk. A key difference, however, is the rear part of the frame, which is only rudimentary. This grip stub replaces the large square grip frame and makes it possible to add a special grip: a combination of a bulky soft rubber grip with side wood trim, which is non-slip, cushions recoil, and also deals with the "case trick" by means of a longer screw and wider slot. It also looks fine. No wonder that Sturm, Ruger here took a loan for the "powerful" Super Redhawk. Incidentally, the frame is a full scale reduction of the Redhawk frame, with a bridge cross section of 17.4 x 6.5 (RH 18 x 7) millimeters, comparable material savings in the crane section, and a 40.2 (RH 46.2) millimeter high and 44.7 (RH 48.7) millimeter wide cylinder window – in short, medium-sized and, despite the flat 120 degree grip angle, also can be gripped by smaller hands.

Launched in 1986, the GP-100 series only followed the then-contemporary taste in its appearance. Technically, the Ruger middle class models are based largely on the Redhawk concept of 1979. In the photo, the "elongated" KGP-161 in front of the kept-short GP-160 – investment casting in stainless steel and blued.

The six shot cylinder, except for the seal ring under the chamber mouths, corresponds to the large cylinder; it is made smaller only in terms of caliber. The diameter is 39.3 (RH 45.2) millimeters and length 41 (RH 44.5) millimeters; it is set on the hollow shaft of the crane, which locks in the frame, and the 2.2 millimeter offset of the locking groove guarantees a minimal gap of the chamber bores from the cylinder. The cylinder has the same accessories and is emptied with the axially offset ejector rod. As with the Redhawk, when the hammer is cocked, end and lateral play are hardly noticeable. A similarly tight play between locking groove and lever, is somewhat lost in the side play of the lever on the frame side.

The trigger unit, its bearing and the trigger action parts mounted in the frame, represent a mix of the .357 trigger system, which was overhauled in 1973 and the Redhawk, in line with the less generous space of the new design. As a result, the module, fitted forward in the frame extends far to the rear with a cast-on bridge with integral locking pin, to compensate for the distance of the trigger guard from the narrow grip frame. It contains, besides the adopted parts, a trigger spring in "personal union" with the locking pin spring, and a shorter lever to rotate the cylinder and for the firing pin safety. The mainspring, again independent, stretches upwards diagonally from the grip frame and acts directly

Not the same, but similar: Separate springs for trigger and hammer replace the central spring/cocking lever arrangement of the older design; the square butt is replaced by a much-reduced grip frame. The solid frame, the trigger mechanism inserted from below, and the unusual cylinder lock were retained.

on the hammer, via the rod. Anyone who might tentatively take to an investment casting with a diamond file, will be surprised by the hardness of the parts. All surfaces and angles are ground flat and sharp. Trigger and hammer show no above-average bearing play. Nevertheless, in single action, the tip of the GP-100 trigger does not come precisely from the cock notch – the cocked trigger mechanism still needs to be pulled. During cocking, the track-less hammer compresses the mainspring, catches the sear under the tip and pulls the trigger until it clicks backwards. Simultaneously, the trigger releases the cylinder stop, and turns the cylinder by the right-attached pawl left to the next chamber, lifting the left hinged transfer bar in front of the firing pin, and releases the cylinder stop to re-engage. The whole process is so calculated, that the cylinder comes to a standstill well before, and the hammer strut stops, as the hammer clicks into place. The drop of the hammer and returning trigger make the mechanism reset. In double action, the trigger mechanism operates perfectly smoothly. Without any noticeable transition, the hammer shifts from the moveable catch to the fixed sear, and notches to the cylinder on the cocking lever only after some delay. Despite the high pull weight of about 50 Newtons, it is possible to get a fast rate of fire with sufficient precision.

The slim grip frame not only fits with a plump soft rubber grip, but also creates space for the enclosed trigger spring and the locking bolt spring loaded with it in the trigger unit.

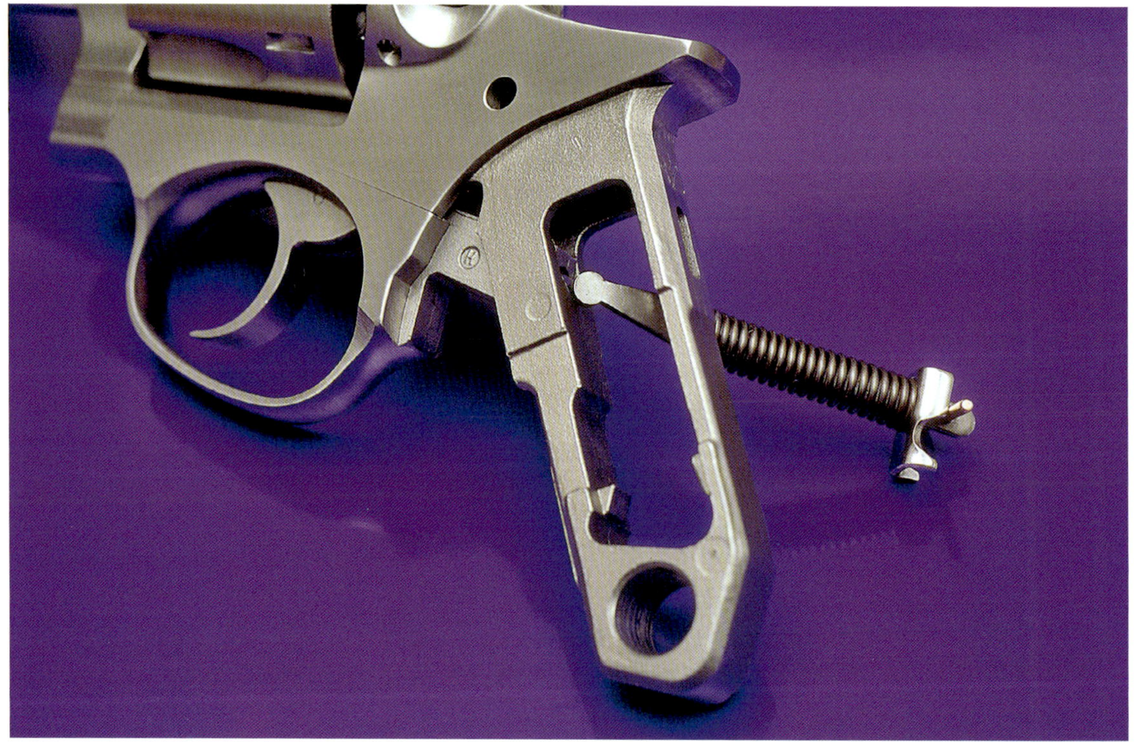

Like the Redhawk spring tension lever, the GP-100 mainspring rod can be used to remove the trigger unit. This is how the locking bolt is pushed from the frame bores.

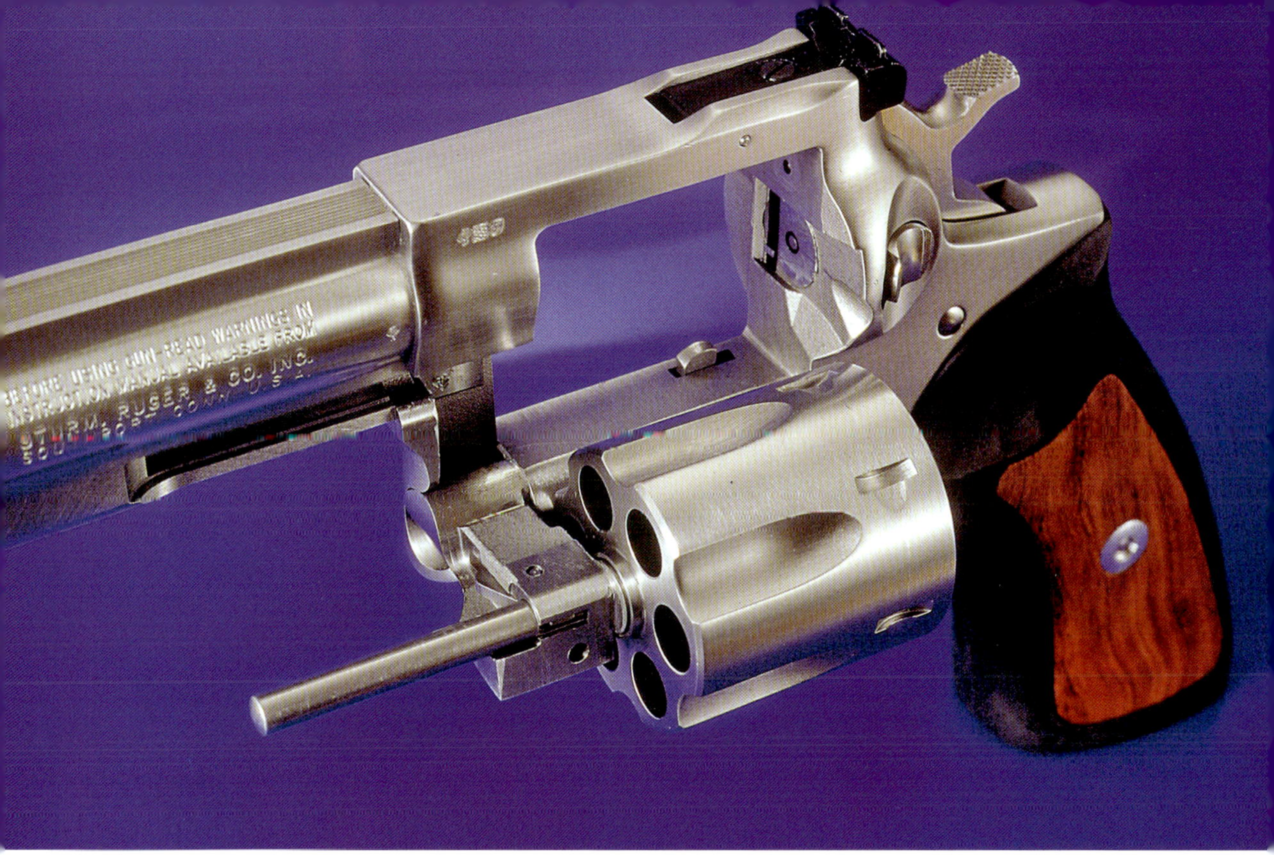

Everything one size smaller: cylinder lock in .357 scale.

Sturm, Ruger importer Frankonia offered, respectively, the six-inch blued GP-100 as catalogue model GP-160 with a short underlug, and the rust-resistant version as KGP-161 with a long underlug in 2005 and 2009. Short and long version are made in one piece with barrel and barrel rib; in terms of appearance, the long version effectively incorporates its 75 grams of extra weight with flowing transitions and the beveled muzzle area. Barrel length is consistently 152 millimeters. Both versions include five right-twist grooves with a twist length of 476 millimeters, an 11 degree forcing cone, and a well-recessed muzzle. On the barrel rib, the Redhawk front sight saddle was eliminated to bypass the frame height, so that the otherwise identical sight is set three millimeters lower. Rear and front sights differ only in width and by the solid black ramp front sight.

Frankonia Freestyle 1500

With the GP-100 series, the importer also went to the tuners. From 1998 to 2009, the frame and trigger mechanism of the solid Standard model were used as the basis of a special series, the Frankonia Master Line, designed to take basically all stationary and dynamic revolver events into consideration. Freestyle is the all-rounder, compact and lightweight enough for most challenges. The names of the Target Master and 357 Practical show what they are intended for. The pictured Freestyle 1500 represented the high requirements of PPC (Practical Police Course) shooting. For this purpose, the pre-loading Six Shooter, ready for delivery with Aristocrat sights in three programmable settings, demonstrates its advantage not in its special qualities for target shooting, but because of the tangible and measurable improvement of its trigger mechanism action with relatively simple means. The completely reliable TriggerScan system

registered with the original mainspring, a remarkable reduction of pull weight just due to the further processing of the serial parts. In single action, the rounded sear of the hammer already reduced cocking resistance, and when a shot is fired, the cock notch, shortened from 0.4 to 0.25 millimeters, on the back side of the sear and the articulated edge of the notch surface on the trigger tip, work so perfectly together, that the trigger releases the cocked hammer at just 14.71 Newton (GP-160: 27.71 Newton). The same finishing touches also include the sliding surface of the trigger lip and cocking lever, which engage alternately under the movable and fixed hammer catch in double action, and the catches themselves. The hammer lifter, with a slightly altered profile, slides longer to the trigger tip, where the sear, 0.5 millimeters shorter, engages in the cocking lever already at 38.25 Newton (GP-160: 42.92 Newton). The tuned double action trigger scores higher in the trigger pull profiles.

Special model Freestyle 1500 from the Frankonia Master Line. The PPC revolver is a modified GP-100 in stainless steel with heavy target barrel (Bull Barrel), programmable Aristocrat sight, and reworked trigger mechanism.

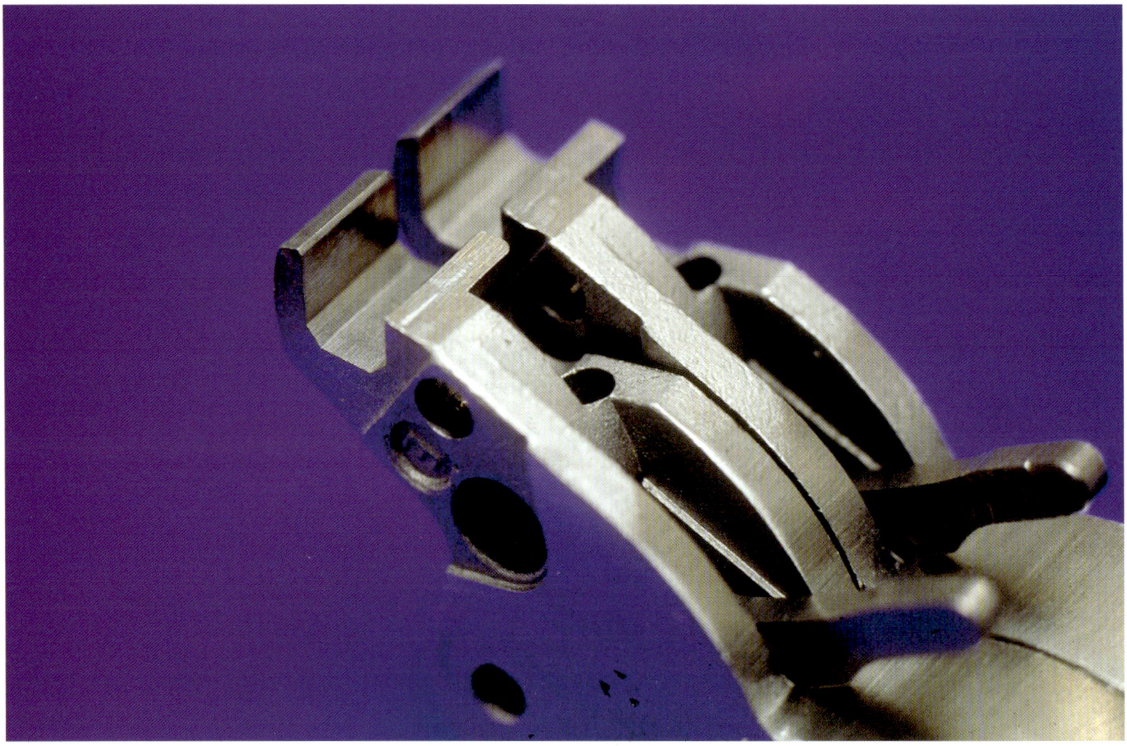

Freestyle and mass-produced triggers compared: chamfered tip to facilitate exit from the notch and smoothed spring to reduce pull weight.

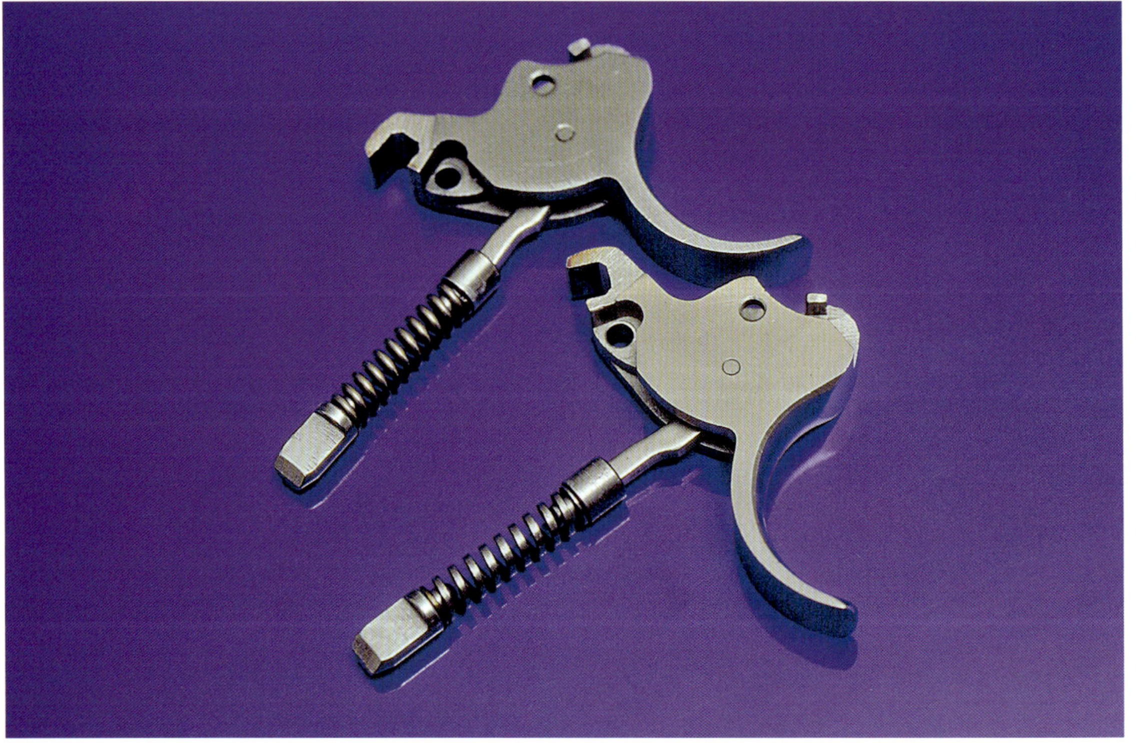

Series SP-101

Sturm, Ruger launched the short-barreled Series SP-101 in 1989, with the catalog models KSP-821 (2 1/4 inches) and KSP-831 (3 1/16 inches) in .38 Special. The small caliber KSP-221 (2 1/4 inches) and KSP-241 (4 inches) followed in 1990, and between 1991 to 1993, came the KSP-3231 (3 1/16 inches) in .32 H&R Magnum, the KSP-921 (2 1/4 inches) and KSP-931 (3 1/16 inches) in 9 mm Parabellum, the KSP-321 (2 1/4 inches) and KSP-331 (3 1/16 inches) .357 Magnum/.38 Special. The double-action-only versions KSP-821 L, KSP-831 L and KSP-321 XL were mass-produced between 1991 and 1993. All the models in this wide-ranging production series with all its different types were, and are, manufactured in stainless steel. Three of the more recent versions are five-shot models (KSP-331 X, KSP-931, KSP-821 L); the others are six-shot. For the sights, there is either a cutout in the frame bridge, or an only-for-windage adjustable rear sight, both behind a flat ramp front sight. Finally, an added X designates Magnum models with elongated frame and longer barrel (KSP-321 X, KSP-321 XL, KSP-331 X). This longer version allows the manufacturer to get beyond the limitation imposed by the barrel of the original .357, which kept bullet weight 125 grains and cartridge length up to only 1.57 inches.

Rounded sear arm and shortened cock notch on the Freestyle hammer.

Mini Magnum: KSP-331 X

The KSP-331 X is one of the Magnums which can shoot not only .38 Special and .38 Special + P ammunition assembly, but also "all standard factory .357 loads." Beyond this, frame and barrel length make no difference. Standard and X models are typical of the SP-101 series, with a small frame compared to the medium and large GP-100, Redhawk and Super Redhawk frames. Essentially, they reflect the entire process of double-action revolver development at Sturm, Ruger. The center point remains the solid frame without a side plate, because the trigger id inserted from the bottom, and the transfer bar safety lock. In this model, however, the frame is made on the newer design, and the trigger mechanism has separate trigger- and mainsprings. The grip stub allows use of the now compulsory soft rubber grip, with a pocket for the mainspring pin that makes tool-less gun care possible. Only the side grip inserts are made of plastic.

Like the smaller trigger system, the "historic" back-extending cylinder locking bar, and the rod to compress and release the crane bolt, come off as rather delicate. However, the fittings are in no way inferior to the tight tolerances of the larger versions. The cylinder itself differs from the six shot version with its thinner walls (1.7 millimeter) and elimination of the maintenance-friendly collar for the bearing cover on the front side.

For either service or hunting use, the KSP-331 X has a milled rear sight, a hammer with a lower spur, and 78-millimeter barrel. In front of the clean-cut 3.8-millimeter rectangular rear sight, a long groove, nearly twice as wide, which under certain lighting conditions counteracts against bothersome vignetting; further front, an extremely flat quickdraw front sight allows for rapid readiness to fire from pocket or holster. The barrel, the indicated barrel rib and the long underlug, are all, like the rust-resistant barrel unit, all manufactured as one piece.

You can't put anything over on this one: the KSP-331 X with elongated frame and the same cylinder as the small frame series SP-101, has a barrel which does away with the need to limit projectile weight to 125 grains and cartridge length to 1.57 inches.

Cylinder diameter, still the same as the original model, limits capacity to five cartridges.

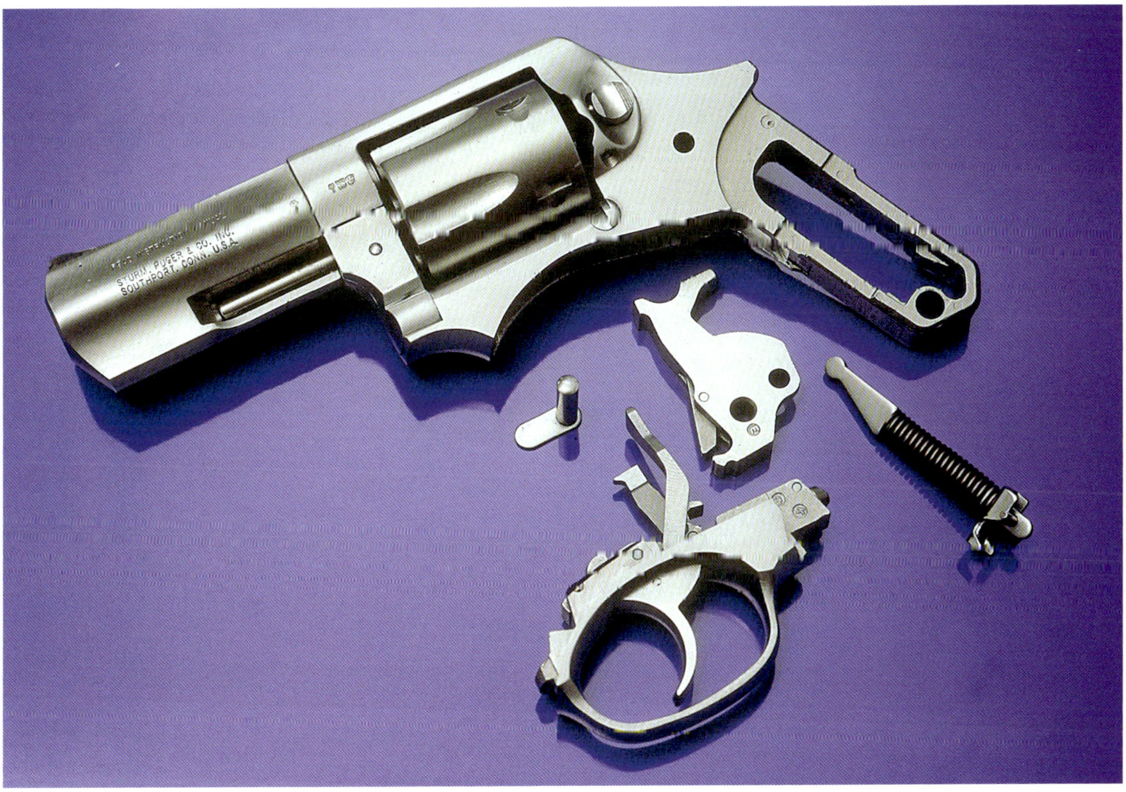

The parts of the either small or medium frames are not compatible, although they are very similar.

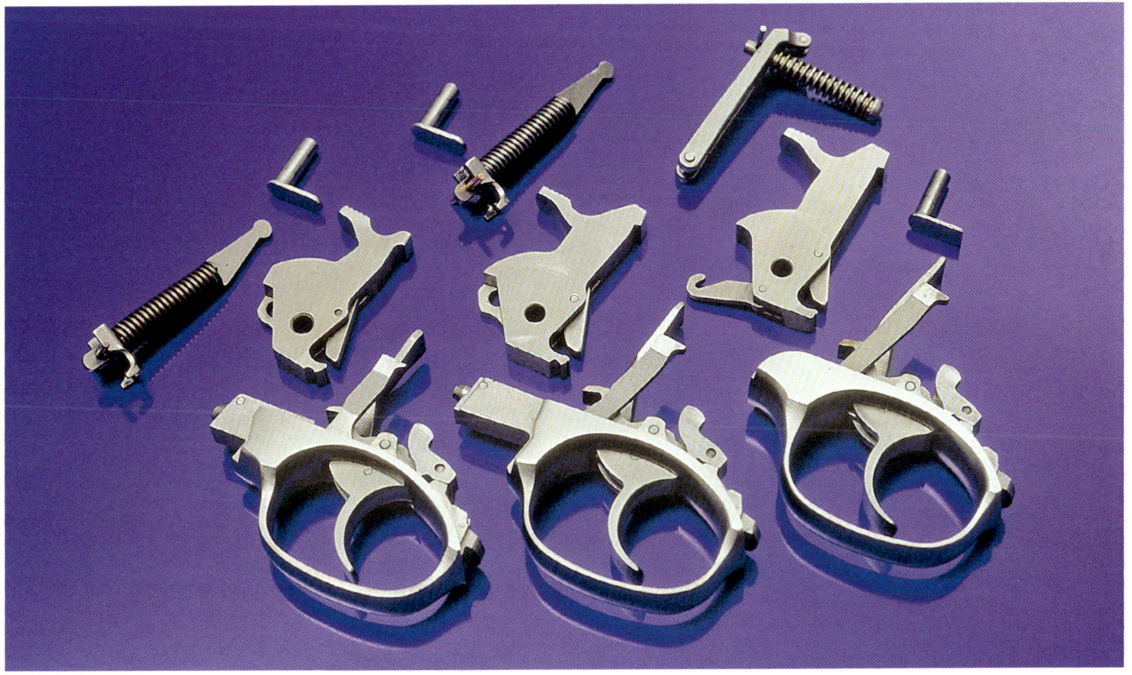

Trigger units in their respective size gradations, by series: SP-101 (left), GP-100, and RH (Redhawk).

Sturm, Ruger in Germany*

Importers	Frankonia Handels-GmbH & Co. KG, Rottendorf, Germany					
Model	**Version**	**Caliber**	**Barrel length**	**Cylinder capacity**	**Weight****	**Price (incl. VAT)**
KP-90 D	LM/ Stainless steel	.45 Colt	4 1/2"/114 mm	6 cartridges	about 1,200 g	€ 719 (2005)
KP-90 D Compact	LM/ Stainless steel	9 mm Parabellum	3 9/10/79 mm	6 cartridges	about 1,150 g	€ 719 (2005)
KGP-160 (Series GP-100)	Stainless steel	.357 Magnum/ .38 Special	6"/152 mm	6 cartridges	about 1,150 g	€ 719 (2005)
KGP-161 (Series GP-100)	Stainless steel	.357 Magnum/ .38 Special	6"/152 mm	6 cartridges	1,255 g	€ 649 (2009)
GP-160 (Series GP-100)	Investment casting, blued	.357 Magnum/ .38 Special	6"/152 mm	6 cartridges	1,180 g	€ 699 (2005)
GP-161 (Series GP-100)	Investment casting, blued	.357 Magnum/ .38 Special	6"/152 mm	6 cartridges	about 1,200 g	€ 699 (2005)
GP-141 (Series GP-100)	Investment casting, blued	.357 Magnum/ .38 Special	4"/102 mm	6 cartridges	about 1,000 g	€ 719 (2005)
KGP-141 (Series GP-100)	Stainless steel	.357 Magnum/ .38 Special	4"/102 mm	6 cartridges	about 1,000 g	€ 649 (2009)
KGPF-331 (Series SP-101)	Stainless steel	.357 Magnum/ .38 Special	3"/76 mm	6 cartridges	about 950 g	€ 649 (2009)
KSP-331 X (Series SP-101)	Stainless steel	.357 Magnum/ .38 Special	3 1/16"/78 mm	5 cartridges	775 g	€ 629 (2009)
KSP-221 (Series SP-101)	Stainless steel	.22 l.r.	2 1/4"/57 mm	6 cartridges	ca. 900 g	€ 659 (2005)
KSP-241 (Series SP-101)	Stainless steel	.22 l.r.	4"/102 mm	6 cartridges	ca. 900 g	€ 659 (2005)
KSP-931 (Series SP-101)	Stainless steel	9 mm Parabellum	3 1/16"/78 mm	5 cartridges	ca. 800 g	€ 679 (2005)
KSP-821 L (Series SP-101)	Stainless steel, DAO trigger	.38 Special	2 1/4"/57 mm	5 cartridges	ca. 780 g	€ 679 (2005)
KRH-445	Stainless steel	.44 Magnum/ .44 Special	5 1/2"/140 mm	6 cartridges	1,375 g	€ 879 (2009)
KRH-44	Stainless steel	.44 Magnum/ .44 Special	7 1/2"/190 mm	6 cartridges	about 1,480 g	€ 929 (2005)

KSRH-7480	Grey/ Stainless steel	.480 Ruger	7 1/2"/190 mm	6 cartridges	about 1,480 g	€ 1,079 (2005)
KSRH-7454	Grey/ Stainless steel	.454 Casull	7 1/2"/190 mm	6 cartridges	about 1,480 g	€ 1,079 (2005)
KSRH-7	Stainless steel	.44 Magnum/ .44 Special	7 1/2"/190 mm	6 cartridges	about 1,480 g	€ 839 (2007)
KSRH-9	Stainless steel	.44 Magnum/ .44 Special	9 1/2"/241 mm	6 cartridges	about 1,600 g	€ 839 (2007)

* Updated range/program and prices under www.henke-online.de
** Manufacturer's information

Frankonia Special Models

Model	Version	Caliber	Barrel length	Cylinder capacity	Weight*	Price (incl. VAT)
Target Master (Series GP-100)	Stainless steel	.357 Magnum/ .38 Special	6"/152 mm	6 cartridges	about 1,150 g	€ 899 (2007)
357 Practical (Series GP-100)	Stainless steel, Bushnell Holosight	.357 Magnum/ .38 Special	6"/152 mm	6 cartridges	about 1,300 g	€ 2,399 (2001)
Freestyle (Series GP-100)	Investment casting, blued	.357 Magnum/ .38 Special	5 1/4"/133 mm	6 cartridges	1,075 g	€ 1,239 (2003)
Freestyle (Series GP-100)	Stainless steel	.357 Magnum/ .38 Special	5 1/4"/133 mm	6 cartridges	1,075 g	€ 1,299 (2003)
Freestyle 1500 (Series GP-100)	Stainless steel	.357 Magnum/ .38 Special	6"/152 mm	6 cartridges	1,780 g	€ 1,299 (2004)
Match Master (Series GP-100)	Stainless steel	.357 Magnum/ .38 Special	6"/152 mm	6 cartridges	about 1,300 g	€ 929 (2005)
Match Master Luxus (Series GP-100)	Stainless steel, Nill target Grip	.357 Magnum/ .38 Special	6"/152 mm	6 cartridges	about 1,300 g	€ 1,169 (2009)
Shark (Series GP-100)	Stainless steel	.357 Magnum/ .38 Special	6"/152 mm	6 cartridges	about 1,150 g	€ 1,399 (2009)

* Manufacturer's information

Sturm-Ruger KSP-331-X/3 inch and KRH-445 Redhawk / 5 1/2 inch, Technical Specifications and Prices

Manufacturer	Sturm, Ruger & Company Inc., Southport, Connecticut, U.S.A.	
Series/ Catalog model	**SP-101/KSP-331 X**	**KRH-445 Redhawk**
Caliber	.357 Magnum/.38 Special	.44 Magnum/.44 Special
Version	Stainless steel, cast, polished, brushed. Fluted barrel	
Weight	775 g	1,375 g
Cylinder capacity	5 cartridges	6 cartridges
Length	200 mm	277 mm
Width	34.3 mm	45.2 mm
Height	120 mm	150 mm
Trigger-backstrap distance	SA 62 mm DA 72 mm	SA 72 mm DA 82 mm
Grip angle	120 degrees	110 degrees
Grip	Soft rubber/plastic	Rosewood, classic design
Barrel	78 mm, five grooves, right twist	140 mm, six grooves, right twist
Cylinder diameter	34.3 mm	45.2 mm
Cylinder length	40.3 mm	44.5 mm
Cylinder gap	0.18 mm	0.1 mm
Trigger pull weight*	SA 25.06 N/2.56 kp DA 52.12 N/5.32 kp	SA 26.13 N/2.64 kp DA 43.22 N/4,41 kp
Sight length/ line of sight over the barrel axis	119 mm/15 mm	183 mm/23 mm
Rear sight width/ front sight width	3.8 mm/3.2 mm	3.5 mm/3.5 mm
Price incl. VAT	629 euros (2009)	879 euros (2009)

*TriggerScan measurements

Sturm, Ruger GP-100/6 inch, Technical Specifications and Prices

Manufacturer	Sturm, Ruger & Company Inc., Southport, Connecticut, U.S.A.		
Model	**GP-100/GP-160**	**GP-100/KGP-161**	**Cap GP-100/ Frankonia Freestyle 1500**
Caliber	.357 Magnum/.38 Special		
Version	Stainless steel, cast, polished, brushed. Hard chrome plated barrel shroud. Fluted barrel	Steel (blued)	Stainless steel
Weight	1,180 g	1,255 g	1,780 g
Cylinder capacity	6 cartridges		
Length	294 mm	294 mm	295 mm
Width	39.3 mm	39.3 mm	39.3 mm
Height	143 mm	143 mm	152 mm
Trigger-backstrap distance	SA 72 mm DA 82 mm	SA 72 mm DA 82 mm	SA 73 mm DA 83 mm
Grip angle	120 degrees		
Grip/grip panels	Soft rubber/wood		
Barrel	152 mm, five grooves, right twist	152 mm, five grooves, right twist	152 mm, polygon, six segments right twist
Cylinder diameter	39.3 mm	39.3 mm	39.3 mm
Cylinder length	41 mm	41 mm	41 mm
Cylinder gap	0.15 mm	0.15 mm	0.12 mm
Trigger pull weight*	SA 27.71 N/2.83 kp DA 52.32 N/5.34 kp	SA 23.76 N/2.42 kp DA 47.64 N/4.86 kp	SA 14.71 N/1.50 kp DA 45.36 N/4.63 kp
Sight length/ line of sight over the barrel axis	190 mm/20 mm	190 mm/20 mm	199 mm/31 mm
Rear sight width/ front sight width	3.0 mm/3.5 mm	3.5 mm/3.2 mm	2.7 mm/3.2 mm
Price incl. VAT	699 euros (2005)	649 euros (2009)	1,299 euros (2004)

*TriggerScan measurements

Trigger Pull Profile [N/mm]

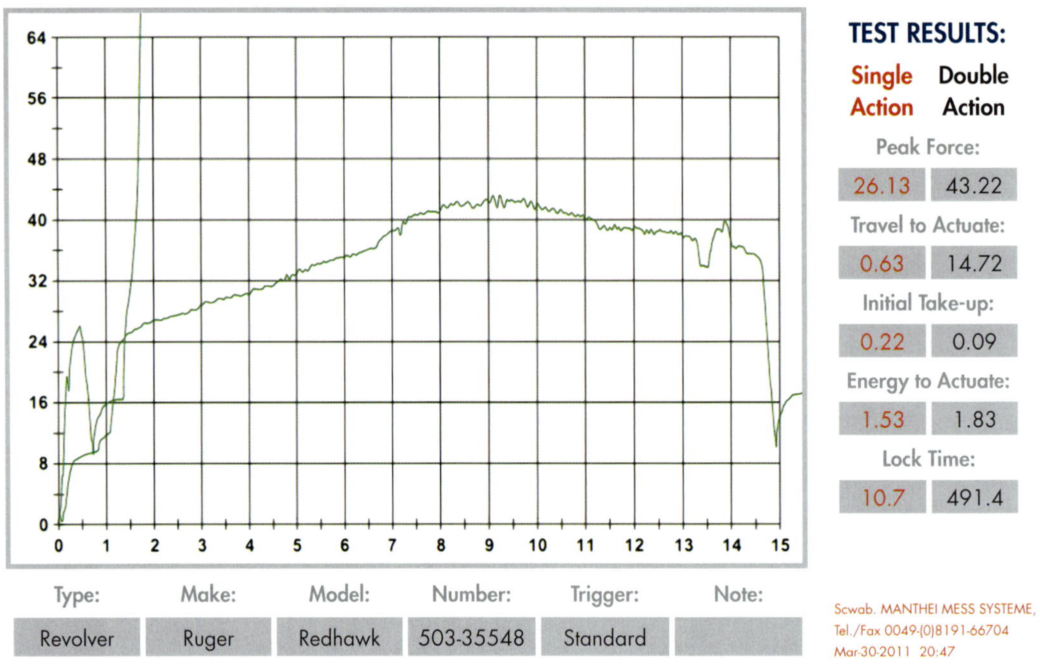

KRH-445 Redhawk

Trigger Pull Profile [N/mm]

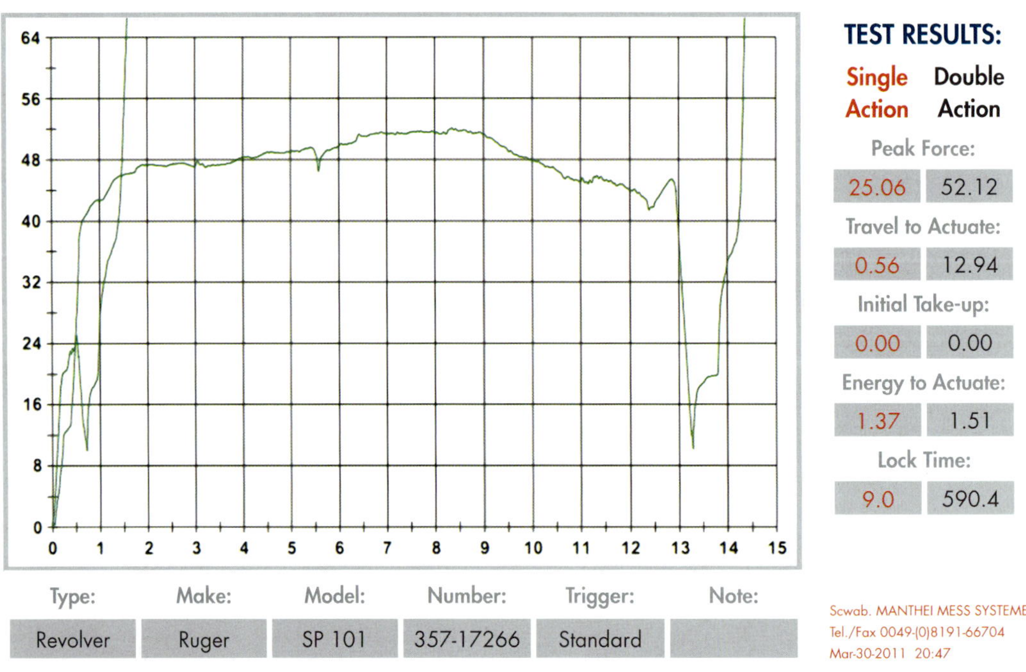

SP-101/KSP-331 X

Trigger Pull Profile [N/mm]

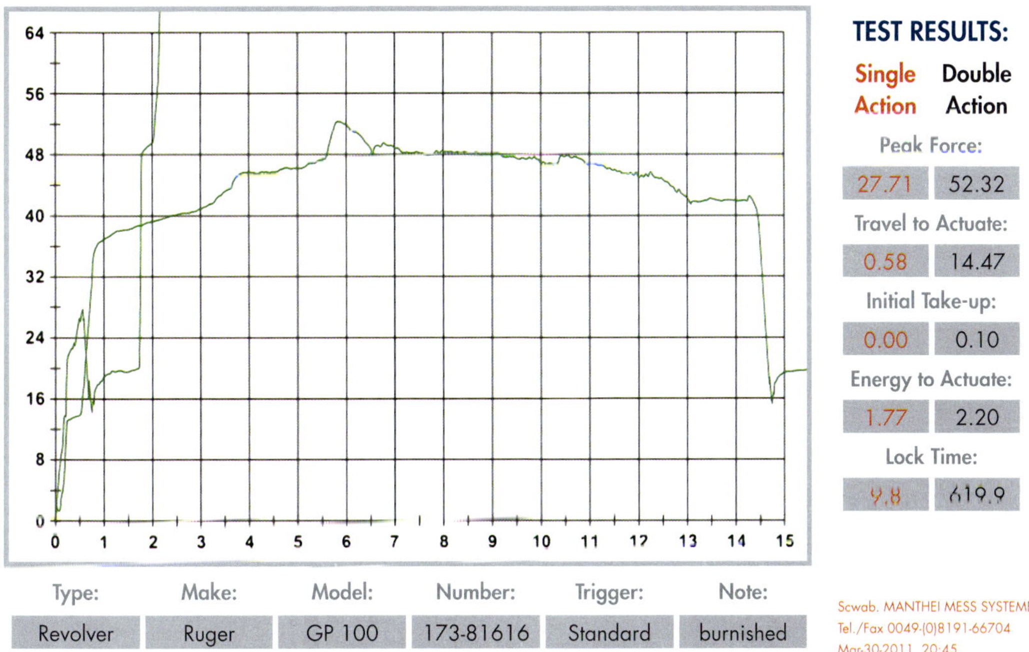

GP-100/GP-160

Trigger Pull Profile [N/mm]

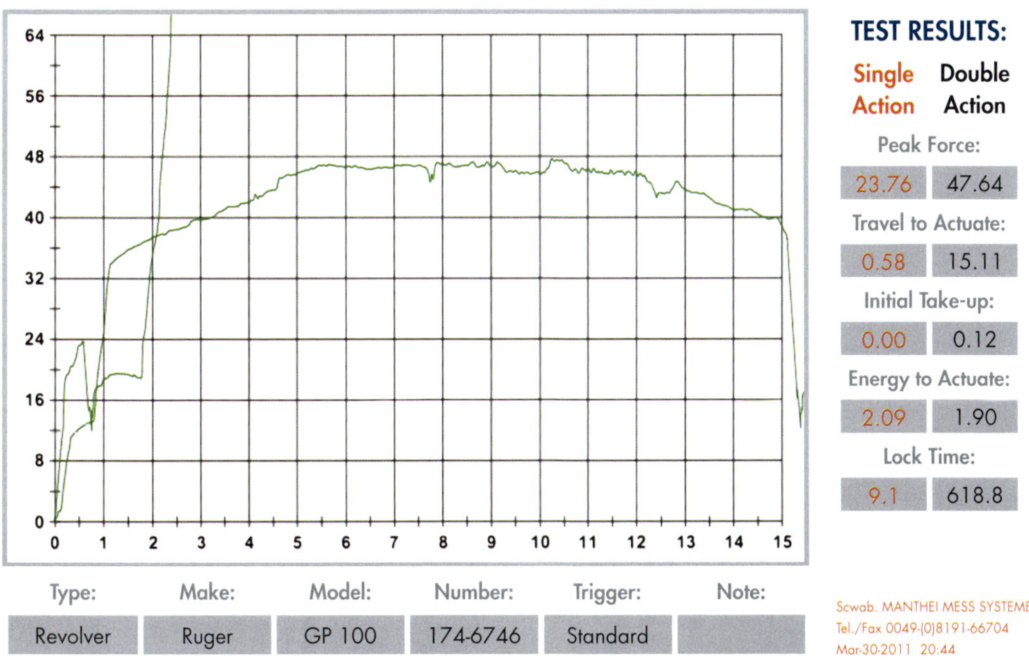

GP-100/KGP-161

Trigger Pull Profile [N/mm]

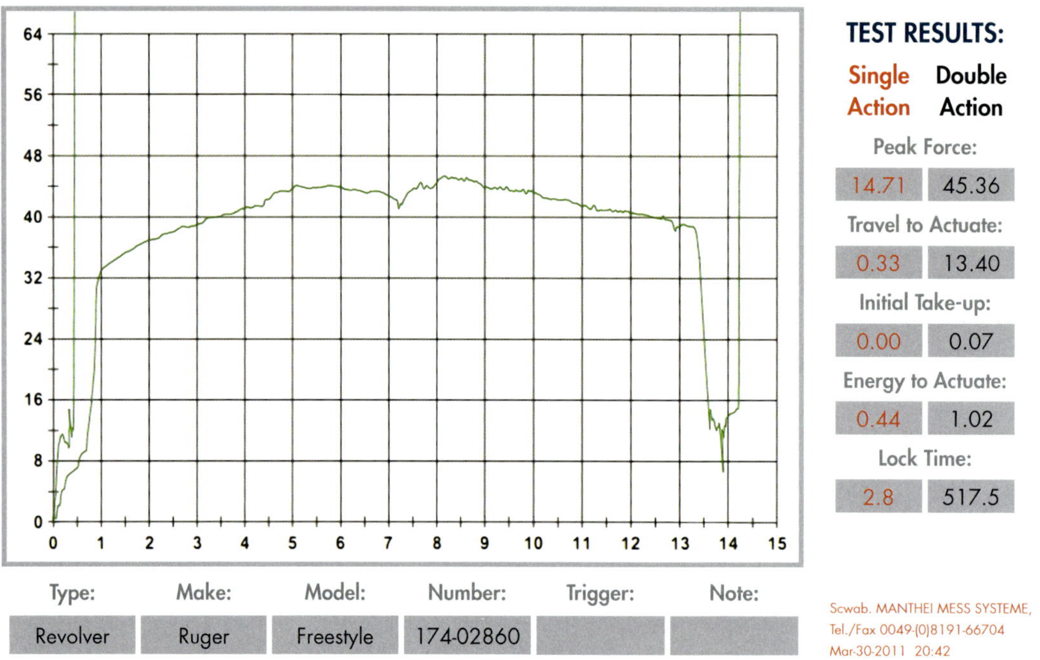

TEST RESULTS:

	Single Action	Double Action
Peak Force:	14.71	45.36
Travel to Actuate:	0.33	13.40
Initial Take-up:	0.00	0.07
Energy to Actuate:	0.44	1.02
Lock Time:	2.8	517.5

Scwab. MANTHEI MESS SYSTEME,
Tel./Fax 0049-(0)8191-66704
Mar-30-2011 20:42

GP-100 Frankonia Freestyle 1500

Taurus

Artistic Metalwork from Brazil

Nomen est omen: *Forjas* (Portuguese) means "forge" or "blacksmith's worshop"; in Porto Alegre, in the state of Rio Grande do Sul, the Brazilian company Forjas Taurus SA hammer-drop forges the frames and other parts of their usually large-caliber steel and titanium revolvers. In the era of increasing rationalization, it is only possible to use such an elaborate process and do the required post-processing work in low-wage countries – unless the manufacturer has a clientele that appreciates quality materials and excellent workmanship, as well as perfectly functioning weapons, and will pay prices for all this comparable to those commanded by Korth or Janz.

This Brazilian firearms maker has been producing their guns since 1939, using a distinct reference to Smith & Wesson, yet not always faithful to their model. As a result, there are many similarities in overall design and frame sizes, but at the same time, the cylinder bearing, cylinder lock and trigger mechanism all display all kinds of distinct details. Smith & Wesson, for example, has eliminated the indent for the swing-out cylinder, the so-called "tear drop," on the frame of its newer models; it is replaced by an internal support system. Regardless of model, frame, or cylinder size, this system is based on the slotted sprung claw socket in the base of the cylinder, which extends from the hollow shaft of the crane. There are four claws in the mating cone of the shaft bore, and when the ejector rod is inserted, cannot rebound open. To dismantle the revolver, it is only necessary to remove these and the cylinder can be pulled from the hollow shaft, against the spring action of the claws. The cylinder itself is mounted directly on the hollow shaft and is supported by a thrust ring, which is also part of the shaft seal, and kept at a distance from the crane.

The two-part, double spring loaded ejector rod turns with the spindle in the crane and rotates with the cylinder. The frictional connection, and thus force transmission from the cylinder pawl the ejector star teeth, is created by the profiled star hub, the inner profile of the sprung claw socket, and two pins in the cylinder base. The rod is quite short, and this is unfortunately noticeable when the cases are ejected – on various models, its length is barely two thirds that of a cartridge case.

To lock the cylinder, the new series' ejector rod works only on one side. As with the Smith & Wesson locking rod, a strong spring loaded locking bolt catches in the center of the cylinder plate from the star hub, and activates the weaker spring-loaded cylinder release slide piece for use. In contrast, Taurus moved the front lock from the underside of the barrel to the crane; this has a snap lock which, depending on the model, latches in the frame below the barrel threading as a beveled spring bolt or fixed bolt. The weaker release is opened with one hand, and preferably used in the small and medium magnums, such as the short-barreled 617 Ti and the six-inch 669 and 689 VR (ventilated rib). The stronger version, for the large-frame models such as Raging Bee (.218 Bee), Raging Hornet (.22 Hornet), Raging Thirty (.30 Carbine), and Raging Bull (.41 Magnum, .44 Magnum, .454 Casull and .480 Ruger) features an additional cylinder release latch on the crane, which, since is there is no Ruger-style automatic, must be used along with the frame-bound slide for two-handed action. Crane and cylinder bearing, and the crane lock with its ingrained indent, display clean workmanship and minimal assembly clearance.

Without significantly altering the frame cutout and cover, Taurus has replaced, in a series of steps, the reset lock still common in Smith & Wesson pieces, with a transfer bar safety. Inside the frames, the rough traces of milling which were frequently complained about in the older models, have given way to cleanly machined and finely peened surfaces, as well as polishing of the same quality on the cylinder window and – to reduce friction from the case bases sliding by – on the inside of the cylinder plate. The frame opens to the right, and the cylinder pawl also engages from the right, resulting in the prototypical left opening and left rotation of the cylinder. The coiled mainspring, a must for Taurus, is installed, depending on the frame size, in either a square butt, round butt or a narrow angular grip frame which can take a multi-part recoil-absorbing soft rubber grip.

As Smith & Wesson does, Taurus also equips their revolvers with a universal lock. The only differences are in the dimensions of the parts, which are based on the size of the frame, and in the execution of hammer in regard to the specific purpose of the guns. Like the Bodyguard and Centennial, the Protector and CIA (Carry It Anywhere) both have mostly or completely concealed hammers; all conventional "doubles" have hammers with non-slip spurs. The hammers are protected against accidents by the integrated "Taurus Security System," which keeps the uncocked hammer locked. In the Double-Action-Only models alone, the hammer is locked or unlocked from the frame by the same method.

The trigger mechanism has no lack of freedom of movement. Trigger, hammer, transfer bar, cylinder pawl, cylinder lock and springs almost disappear into their frame cutouts, although the mechanism, in terms of execution, assembly and kinematics all strongly recall the no-longer-used reset lock. Here also, the trigger carries out the duties of the trigger bar; its tip and cocking lever cock the hammer and trigger; its nose activates the cylinder stop and guides the cylinder pawl and hammer strut sideways. Trigger, hammer, and cylinder stop are smooth or matte investment castings and, in the newer models, are made using the MIM injection molding technique.

The only changes in the action of the mechanism action are in the safeties. In the reset lock, the slide, pressed from the trigger spring, pulls the dropped hammer back just so far when the trigger is released, that the extended hammer block can enter the resulting gap between frame and hammer. However, it is an encased coil spring which does the work in the transfer bar lock. The firing pin is linked to the trigger, moves opposite to the hammer block and transmits the impact impulse to top dead center on the hammer strut. The hammer has a nose for impact and drop safety, when the hammer strut is lowered by the rebounding firing pin, it rests against the frame.

In single action, the whole movement sequence starts when the hammer sear catches under the trigger tip. In older models, the springs are compressed by guide rods with a round profile and ball head, which lie on the hammer and trigger in pans; they are retained in the frame window (mainspring) and on a bolt in the frame cutout (trigger spring). In the new design trigger mechanism, there are flat, hammer spring rods, which, like the other guide rods, have a transverse bore for fixing the pre-tensioned spring. As the hammer turns, the trigger nose pulls the floating cylinder stop up until the cylinder is released from the locking groove, while the trigger, turning backwards, lifts the right-hinged cylinder pawl to the ratchet of the ejector star, and the left hinged hammer strut before the firing pin. At the same time, depending on the model, a pin in the pawl blocks either the single or the rear cylinder release slide, so that the cylinder cannot be swung out when the hammer is cocked. Both cylinder pawl and hammer strut are stamped steel parts. Cocking the hammer ends when the cylinder stop is deflected, after a clear "indication" that the cylinder has rotated further, the tip engages in the cock notch after a lag, and the hammer strut is in contact position to the firing pin. After the shot is fired, the released trigger swings back to the starting position, pulls its positively controlled companion out of its range, and clicks back into the cylinder stop.

In double action, the trigger tip and cocking tooth transfer from the movable hammer catch to the fixed sear, turn the hammer away over the outermost stop point, and, immediately after the cylinder stops, positions it, with hammer strut raised, ready to drop. All other action, including resetting the system with pressure from the trigger spring, are the same as in single action.

Over fifty double action and double-action-only Taurus revolver models are circulating worldwide, made in steel, duralumin, titanium or composite design, and there are more than three times as many versions of all the features available. These include versions which are blued, rust resistant, stainless, and deluxe revolvers, with titanium-treated trigger mechanism parts, and imitation mother of pearl for the grip. There are also five-, six-, seven-, eight- and nine-shot specimens, and those with 2, 2 1/2, 4, 5, 6, 6 1/2, 8 3/8, 10, and 12 inch barrels.

Many of the barrels have gas ports that open in three or four rows next to the front sight. The calibers on offer cover the whole spectrum: .17 HMR (according to Taurus "the best for hunting coyotes, rabbits, squirrels, crows and similar creatures"), .218 Bee, .22 l.r., .22 WMR, .22 Hornet, .30 Carbine, .32 H&R Magnum, .38 Special, .357 Magnum, .41 Magnum, .44 Special, .44 Magnum, .45 Colt, .45 ACP, .454 Casull and .480 Ruger. The 454 Raging Bull was the first swing-out revolver in one of the "super calibers," and later moved Smith & Wesson to introduce its X frame models.

The Blue Wonder: 617 Ti

Anything that can be produced in titanium, is made of titanium, or is – in the trademarked abbreviation – "Total Titanium." This trademark has identified Taurus' titanium pocket revolver since it was introduced at the turn of the millennium, and guarantees that this exotic metal has been used for all components except barrel brushes (barrels), trigger mechanism and its parts, rods, and screws. This material, better known in aerospace and automotive technology, sets limits for hardening, beyond which there is a risk of attrition; all the same, titanium with a density of 4.54 g/cm 3 compared to iron (7.874 g/cm 3), is the ideal material for non-aluminum (2.702 g/cm3)-based lightweight construction. The seven-shot .357 shown weights just 562 grams.

Considering the fact that this tough material is difficult to work with, and that surfaces are even harder to polish, the Bright Spectrum Blue 617 Ti (617 TB 2C) shows a finish in no proportion to its price of well below 1,000 euros. This processed alloy alone costs many times more that the rust-resistant steel usually used for gun making. In terms of machining and fit, both the CNC-machined forged parts such as frames, lock plate, cylinder crane and barrel shroud, and the CNC-turned cylinder and other parts, basically leave nothing to be desired. The outer surfaces are mirror-finished, without being polished round on the corners and edges; the lock plate disappears almost seamlessly into the frame; the cylinder crane follows the exact contours of the frame; and the frame interior displays a high level of workmanship. The stainless steel barrel bushing and titanium casing are

Forestry Chief Inspector Michael Lunkwitz experiences his Blue Wonder. He won't soon forget firing his test shot on the Markendorf moor!

In fact, the Taurus 617 Ti, a short-barreled .357 with a curb weight of just 562 grams, is not easy to master.

ported on either side of the front sight in three V-shaped rows. Taurus calls the package the "steel-sleeved titanium barrel" and certifies the compensator muzzle in titanium for the highest resistance to corrosion and erosion.

The trigger mechanism is also made to high standards. In comparing weight pull profiles, the 617 Ti intersects at 17.01 N in single action, 43.92 N in double action and a very uniform course in both actions, at the level of the tuned 689 Euro Champion – and better than most competing brands. Trigger and hammer match the shimmering blue firearm, and are smoothed and color case hardened.

617 Ti

“Sometimes it takes more than steel, alloys or polymer composites to make the perfect handgun”: this is why Taurus uses hammer-drop forged titanium wherever it allows the feasible hardness – only barrel, trigger mechanism parts, parts of the cylinder lock, and screws are made of hardened chrome molybdenum steel.

Taurus has no problem fully loading its compact service revolver with seven magnum cartridges. A bulky rubber grip is used to dampen the particularly strong rebound of the ultra-lightweight.

It is another question, however, whether or not seven shots in the cylinder are in any way relevant for the weapon carrier or hunter. Firing seven shots in rapid succession in hard Magnum ammunition assembly is a hard task for any shooter. Like all snub noses in this caliber, the externally very smart 617 Ti also recoils mercilessly, despite its "shock-absorbing" rubber grip. The shapely Ribber Grip is attached without screws and can be easily cleaned using an enclosed plastic clip or two credit or bankcards. On the shooting machine, this two incher achieves respectable precision. In the Magnum range, it takes factory cartridges from Winchester (10.2 SJ FP), Fiocchi (10.2 g SJ FP), and Lapua (9.7 g CEPP) so well that it gets groups from 35 to 38 millimeters, and with the .38 World Championship Bullets (10.2 g lead FP) it produces an amazing 29 millimeters. You should be able to take on a wild boar with it.

669 and 689 Euro Champion

Target-shooting revolvers are not the preserve of the Brazilians. Taurus primarily makes revolvers for hunting, where it is allowed to hunt with a handgun to make the kill shot, and – to fill out comprehensive handgun use – for self-defense. At least, in terms of what is on offer, revolvers predominate when the issue is "just for fun": for plinking and varminting, the short-barreled mini-Magnum from caliber .32 H&R Magnum, revolvers for pistol calibers, and the compact .44 in Special and Magnum. Nevertheless, the 669, its derivative the 689 VR, and the Hofmann special model 689 Euro Champion, are serious competitors for all target shooting .357s. Taurus designed the 669, like the Smith & Wesson M 586/686, as a service revolver, with the best features to make a second career. The 669 is a medium-frame model in blued or stainless steel, with all design and qualitative improvements added since the introduction of new Magnum models towards the end of the 1990s. These include relocating the front cylinder lock from the underlug to the cylinder crane. In size comparison, the mid-sized Taurus frames are closest to the Smith & Wesson L frames.

As in all newer design Taurus models, in the 617 Ti the hammer strut secures the uncocked trigger mechanism. Thanks to the well-arranged trigger mechanism technology, the recessed transfer bar and the hammer, resting against the frame by the firing pin, are clearly visible.

The Model 669 is a kind of "Distinguished Combat Magnum" with equally good features for further development as a target revolver. The Brazilians, while barely defeated in quality, can never compete with their U.S. models in terms of acceptance.

The biggest differences are in the hammer, which Taurus makes five millimeters longer to create internal space for the milled-in hammer strut guide; in the length compensation of frame bridge with the base between trigger mechanism and crane bearing; in the reduced frame width from 16.5 to 16 millimeters; and in the square butt with divided window to support the mainspring. However, the material reserves of 4.7 millimeters in the frame walls and 5.5 millimeters in the frame bridge are identical.

The forged frame guides the cylinder crane, which swings out left, with little play and provides a tight fit for the crane locking pin under the barrel threading. Like most revolvers, it can be locked one handed quite easily, using the cylinder release slide and sideways pressure on the cylinder cam at the same time. The

In the cocked 669 trigger mechanism, to transmit the impact impulse, the transfer bar is raised. Cross holes for fixing the springs in the guide rods not only make maintenance easier, but also make it possible, if wanted, to make a quick exchange of the manufacturer's springs with weaker ones from the parts trade.

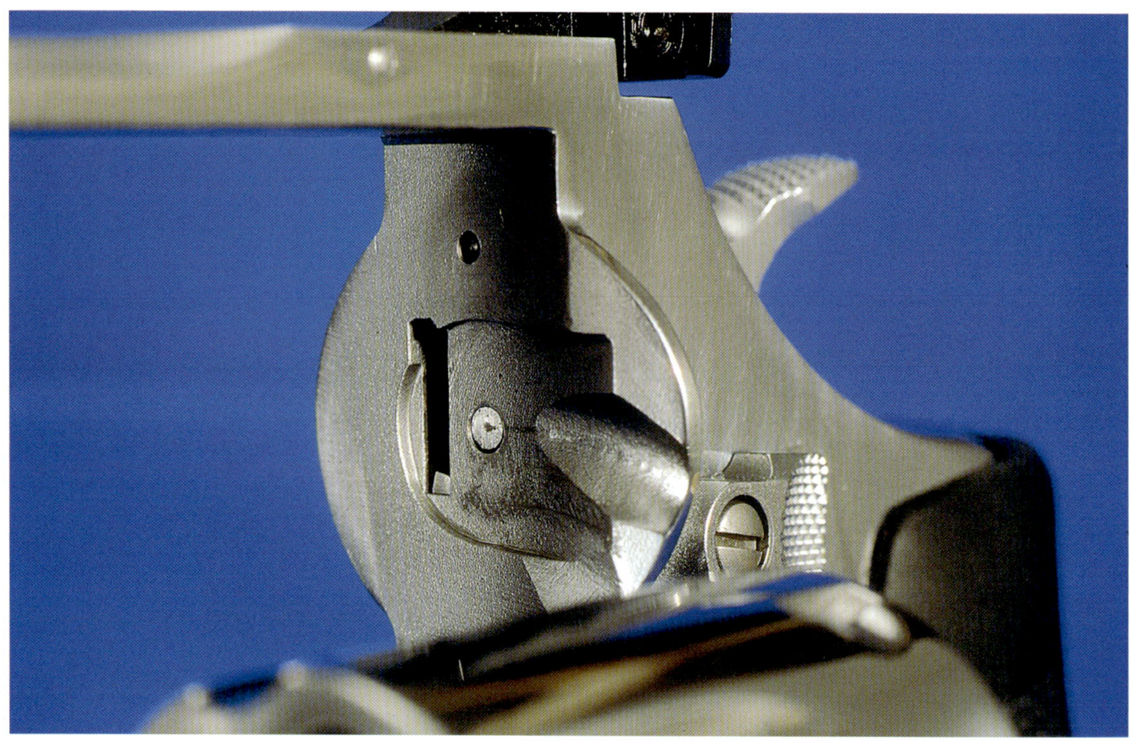

Taurus outfits its double lock models with one- or two-handed release. The 669 has the first type, with the usual lock in the breech face and a spring loaded locking pin on the crane.

left-rotating cylinder is set with the spring claws of the guide bushing in the crane hollow shaft mating cone; the ejector rod secures it from being accidentally detached from the crane. Externally, only the length, at 41.6 millimeters, corresponds to the L frame cylinder (41.3 mm). In diameter, the Taurus is 38, the L frame 39.6 millimeters.

Transfer bar and cylinder pawl are arranged to carry out their dual roles as both transmission elements (hammer strut/cylinder pawl) and safety features (disconnector/safety release), linked left and right on the trigger, so that they neither transmit the impact impulse too early, nor let the cylinder swing out when the hammer is cocked, or allow the back locking bolt, swinging with it, travel over the latch slot in the cylinder plate. In single action, the timing positions- the rotated-up chamber well before, in double action, at the same time, as the dropping hammer behind the barrel. In single action, a slight creep of the trigger is noticeable; this disappeared completely after the tip and notch on the 689 EC (Euro Champion) were reworked. With trigger pull weights of 23.5/21.05 N in single action and 45.06/43.69 N in double action, the 669 and 689 EC are roughly

Hofmann's special model Euro Champion / upgrades the former VR 689 for target shooting with a revamped trigger mechanism and a pinned target front sight on the ventilated rib.

on par with comparable makes. The double-action trigger profile is pleasing; the rest can possibly be accounted for by weaker springs from the parts trade.

Depending on the model, the frame takes a five-times drawn four or six-inch barrel with 476 millimeter right twist. The four- or six-inch Service revolver carries a solid barrel rib; on the exclusively offered six-inch 689 VR and 689 EC, the rib is ventilated and provided to allow screwing on a telescopic sight mount. On all the barrels, the narrow U-shaped underlug extends to the muzzle, where it ends at the slanted angle typical of the brand. In terms of performance, the six-inch misses nothing. At 25 meters, both can easily hit the bull's eye using factory ammunition. The 669 gets the best "run" with a 10.2 gram Magnum ammunition assembly of Geco, Magtech, and WM bullets, each 26 millimeters. For the 689 EC, the Hirtenberger (25 mm), S & B (25 mm) and Federal (29 mm), result in the tightest groups. The shooter can get comparable results with various special ammunition assemblies.

The two models have their differences, however, and these are not only in the response quality of the trigger mechanism and barrel rib mass. The surfaces are also distinct: mirror polished on the 669 and peened to a satin matte on the 689 EC. In terms of execution, the Euro Champion makes an impression with its sharply drawn contours and chiseled edge transitions, while the 669 gives a rounder impression overall. The 689 cylinder release catch has a better ergonomic design; it also has a pinned target front sight, instead of the 669's fixed ramp front sight. The uniform adjustable sight is inscribed and includes a sharply undercut rear sight.

Untamed Bull: 444 Raging Bull

At the 1998 Shot Show in Las Vegas, the .454 Casull Raging Bull launched a revolver series, which can be attributed to borrowings from Smith & Wesson, only to a limited extent. If Forjas Taurus SA was not literally a weapons maker, it could be said that the unbridled bull – later offered in other calibers as 416, 444 and 480 – displays a harmonious design. The trigger mechanism parts, only made for this gun, are cast; more recently using MLM molding technology.

Based on the company philosophy, that its products have the most universal applications as possible, the Raging Bull is mass produced, almost without exception, as compensated revolvers with barrel lengths of 5, 6 1/2, and 8 3/8 inches. Regarding its claims as a firearm for hunting, these beefy revolvers are, according to Taurus advertisements, "simply the best hunting handgun available" – as stated: where games laws allow. One of the few exceptions is the matte silver .44 special model, which importer Hofmann had manufactured lighter and without compensator, in accordance with the regulations of the German *Sportschützenverbände* [Target Shooting Associations]. The barrel length also had to be shortened, from 6 1/2 (165 mm) to a little more than six inches (153 mm).

444 Raging Bull

The one-time award-winning design is still impressive today: Despite the "beefy" construction of the then-strongest caliber .454 Casull, Taurus designed the large frame, elaborate cylinder lock, originally five-shot cylinder, and the solid barrel group to a coherent unit. Importer Hofmann, whose claim for its hunting qualities ("simply the best …") can't be realized in Germany, is focused on its potential for target shooting. He only orders the ported Raging Bull, uncompensated and lighter, as Model 444 in .44 Magnum, as per the regulations of the German Sportschüzenverbände [Target Shooting Associations].

The basis for the award-winning design was the strong initial caliber, which demanded more from the frame, cylinder, and cylinder lock that the trigger weight pull of the 1993 model 44, with the then-largest frame and the usual lock in the center of the cylinder plate and in the underlug. The longer cartridges also imposed their own demands, so that the newcomer was given even more imposing dimensions. It is particularly hefty between the barrel threading and crane bearing, where the crane latches the front of the cylinder with the slide. The frame yoke alone measures 17 x 7 millimeters at its thinnest point, and the frame bridge has notable cross-section dimensions, 16 x 7.5 millimeters. At the back, the frame has a narrow grip stub, designed for a special soft rubber grip. To protect the shooter's middle finger on the trigger guard, the grip goes quite far down; its back has an even softer, bright red rubber insert as additional impact absorber.

Raging Bull in single action: cocked, unlocked, and ready to fire.

The "square" cylinders, each 45 millimeters, rotated in the 49 x 46 millimeter cylinder window. For Casull and Ruger calibers, it is a five-shot and (for the two magnums .41 and .44), a six-shooter. On the five-shot cylinder, the locking grooves lie between the chambers and ensure the strength of the walls for their

1

Raging Bull in double action: Already about to rotate, the trigger makes contact with the hammer lifter via the tip or beak (1), and begins to cock the hammer. Next, the trigger moves from the tip to the cocking lever (2), releases the hammer lifter, engages the hammer under the sear, and finally brings the fully cocked hammer (3) to the highest point, ready to drop. The just-dropped hammer (4) pushes the firing pin from the breech face with the hammer strut.

2

3

4

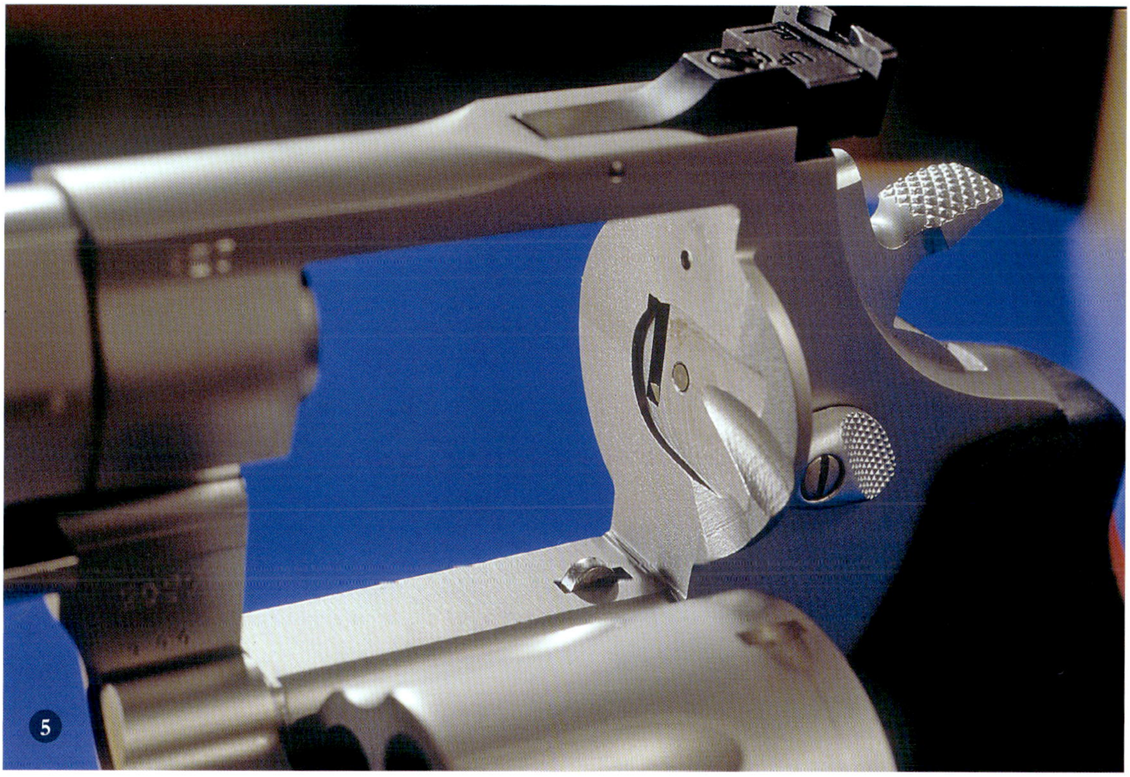

5

The cylinder is locked by the locking bolt of the ejector rod in the center of the cylinder plate, and a slide bar under the barrel threading. Release requires simultaneous – and therefore two-handed – operation of the release slide bar on frame and crane. No problem "theoretically," but a challenge when actually shooting.

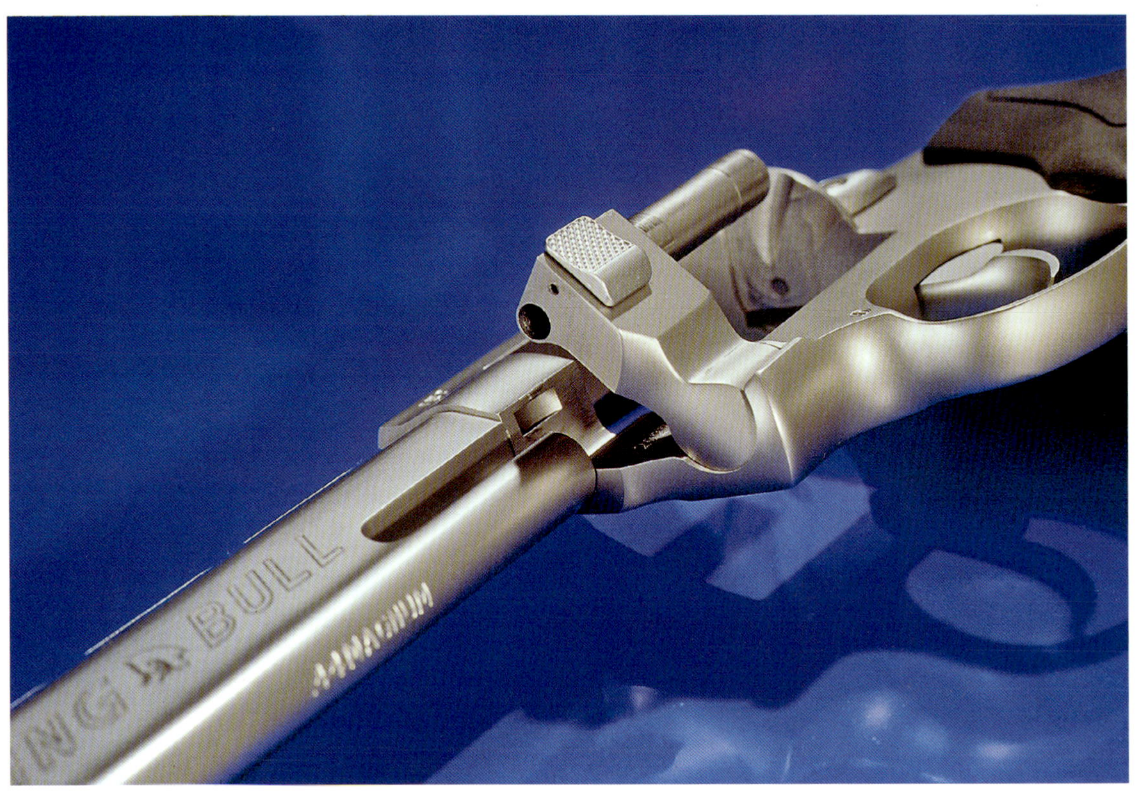

The slide bar latches under the barrel threading.

entire length. In the six-shooter's pitch circle, the 1.4 millimeter deep grooves are directly above the chambers, reducing the .41 cylinder wall thickness from 3.2 to 2.2 millimeters, and that of the .44 to 1.8 millimeters. Cylinder and crane are interconnected by the spring claws of the guide bushing and the two-part ejector rod. The cylinder gap (0.15 mm), cartridge head space (0.35 mm), cylinder end play (0.12 mm), and the more limited play of the crane, lock, and cylinder lock, all reflect Taurus' overall high production standards. The same applies to the timing.

Even more than the massive frame, large cylinder, and special grip, the barrel unit dominates the Raging Bull's impressive exterior. The ported or uncompensated barrel has a striking external profile, with its ventilated rib, muzzle-long underlug, flowing transitions, and the arched muzzle area. This unit has so much mass, that the 6 inch uncompensated version of the 6 1/2

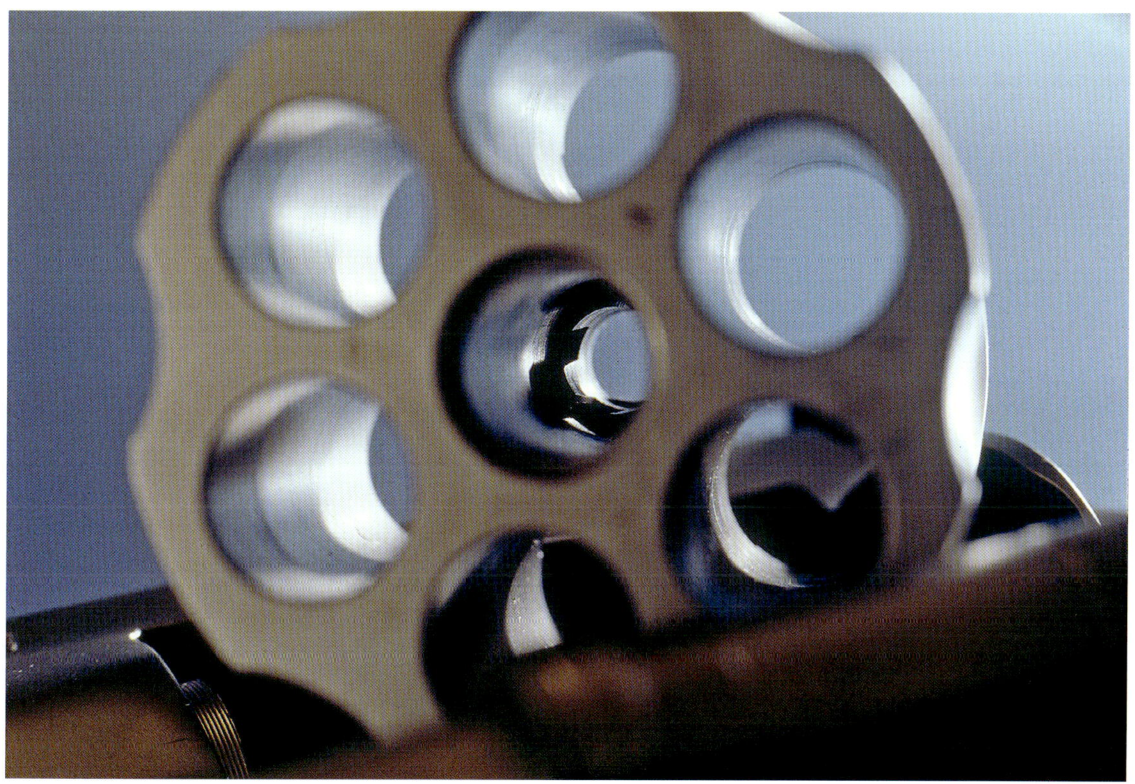

inch .44 barrel, saves the revolver some 68 grams, so that it weighs 1,540 grams, fully compliant to the regulations – the German Shooting Federation allows a maximum weight of 1,550 grams in this caliber. With its recessed muzzle, the shorter barrel has an effective length of 153 millimeters. It has five grooves with 610 millimeter right twist.

For shooters who want to use visual and electronic sights, for general use, hunting, or for special target shooting regulations, this barrel unit has a slotted rail and matching Weaver base, which makes it easy to mount all standard rifle scopes and red dot sights – for target shooting, for example, for the *Bund Deutscher Sportschützen* [German Target Shooters' Association] Free Class. For the open sights, the Raging Bull has the same adjustable sight as models 669 and 689 EC, and a pinned target front sight in the raised front sight saddle.

As in all recent Taurus revolvers, a sprung claw socket controls the cylinder setting on the bearing pin. The inserted ejector rod secures the claws, which are set in the hollow shaft.

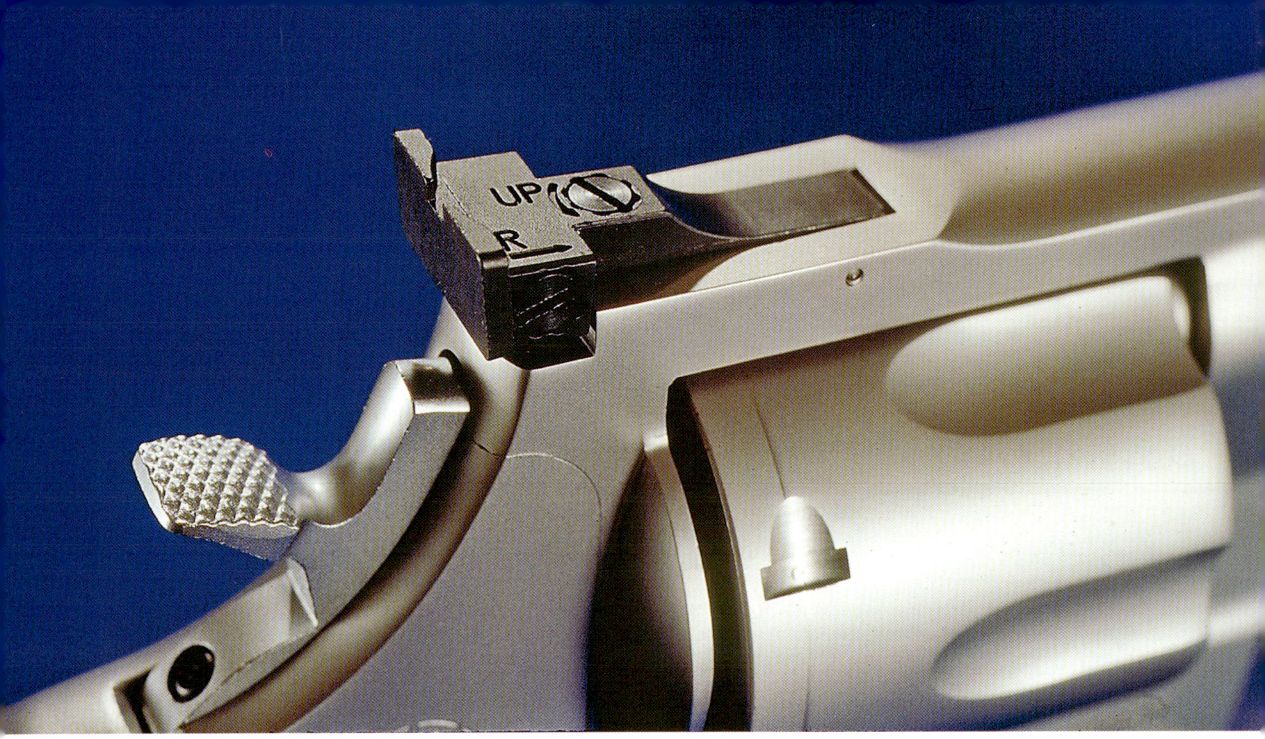

The universally used in-house sight features a sharply undercut rear sight and good quality inscriptions.

Locked up: The patented Taurus Security system blocks the uncocked hammer

Taurus in Germany

Importers	Frankonia Handels GmbH & Co. KG, Rottendorf, Germany Helmut Hofmann GmbH, Mellrichstadt, Germany					
Model	**Version**	**Caliber**	**Barrel length**	**Cylinder capacity**	**Weight***	**Price (incld. VAT)**
605	Stainless steel	.357 Magnum/ .38 Special	2"/51 mm	5 cartridges	700 g	€ 299 (2011)
605 UL	Aluminum/ Stainless steel (matte)	.38 Special	2"/51 mm	5 cartridges	485 g	€ 419 (2004)
617 Ti	Titanium (blue)	.357 Magnum/ .38 Special	2"/51 mm	7 cartridges	562 g	€ 892 (2004)
617 Ti	Titanium (gray)	.357 Magnum/ .38 Special	2"/51mm	7 cartridges	562 g	€ 892 (2004)
Hunter	Stainless steel (matte)	.357 Magnum/ .38 Special	3"/76 mm	5 cartridges	715 g	€ 435 (2011)
Tracker	Stainless steel	.44 Magnum/ .44 Special	4"/102 mm	6 cartridges	980 g	€ 585 (2011)
65	Steel (blued)	.357 Magnum/ .38 Special	4"/102 mm	5 cartridges	1,050 g	€ 370 (2011)
669 Service	Stainless steel (matte)	.357 Magnum/ .38 Special	4"/102 mm	6 cartridges	1,110g	€ 559 2011)
96 EC (Euro Champion)	Stainless steel	.22 l.r.	6"/152 mm	6 cartridges	960 g	€ 499 (2004)
669	Stainless steel	.357 Magnum/ .38 Special	6"/152 mm	6 cartridges	1,225 g	€ 499 (2004)
689 VR	Stainless steel	.357 Magnum/ .38 Special	4"/102 mm	6 cartridges	1,050 g	€ 799 (2000)
689 VR	Stainless steel	.357 Magnum/ .38 Special	6"/152 mm	6 cartridges	1,150 g	€ 799 (2000)
689 EC (Euro Champion)	Stainless steel	.357 Magnum/ .38 Special	6"/152 mm	6 cartridges	1,187 g	€ 599 (2011)
444 Raging Bull	Stainless steel (matte)	.44 Magnum/ .44 Special	6"/153 mm	6 cartridges	1,540 g	€ 725 (2011)

* Manufacturer's information

Taurus 617 Ti/2 inch, 669/6 inch and 689 Euro Champion/6 inch, Technical Specifications and Prices

Manufacturer	Taurus Forjas S.A., Porto Alegre, Brazil		
Model	**617 Ti**	**669**	**689 EC**
Caliber	.357 Magnum/.38 Special		
Version	Titanium, milled, smoothed, polished. Fluted cylinder	Stainless steel, milled, smoothed, polished. Fluted cylinder	Stainless steel, milled, polished, peened. Fluted cylinder
Weight	562 g	1,225 g	1,187 g
Cylinder capacity	7 cartridges	6 cartridges	6 cartridges
Length	182 mm	290 mm	290 mm
Width	38.8 mm	38 mm	38 mm
Height	131 mm	150 mm	149 mm
Trigger-backstrap distance	SA 84 mm DA 75 mm	SA 84 mm DA 75 mm	SA 84 mm DA 75 mm
Grip angle	110 degrees		
Grip/grip panels	Combat, one-piece	Combat, two-piece	Combat, two-piece
Barrel	53.7 mm, five grooves, right twist	152 mm, five grooves, right twist	152 mm, five grooves, right twist
Cylinder diameter	38.8 mm	38 mm	38 mm
Cylinder length	40 mm	41.6 mm	41.6 mm
Cylinder gap	0.2 mm	0.18 mm	0.15 mm
Trigger pull weight*	SA 17.01 N/1.74 kp DA 43.92 N/4.48 kp	SA 23.5 N/2.4 kp DA 45.06 N/4.6 kp	SA 21.05 N/2.15 kp DA 43.69 N/4.46 kp
Sight length/ line of sight over the barrel axis	99 mm/13 mm	226 mm/23 mm	193 mm/22 mm
Rear sight width/ front sight width	3.5 mm/3.0 mm	3.3 mm/3.3 mm	3.3 mm/3.7 mm
Price incl. VAT	892 euros (2004)	499 euros (2004)	599 euros (2011)

*TriggerScan measurements

Taurus Raging Bull 444/6 inch, Technical Specifications and Price

Manufacturer	Taurus Forjas S.A., Porto Alegre, Brazil
Model	**444 Raging Bull**
Caliber	.44 Magnum/.44 Special
Version	Stainless steel, milled, polished, peened. Fluted cylinder
Weight	1,540 g
Cylinder capacity	6 cartridges
Length	302 mm
Width	45 mm
Height	163 mm
Trigger-backstrap distance	SA 81 mm DA 91 mm
Grip angle	115 degrees
Grip/grip panels	Combat, integrated shock absorber
Barrel	153 mm, five grooves, right twist
Cylinder diameter	45 mm
Cylinder length	45 mm
Cylinder gap	0.15 mm
Trigger pull weight*	SA 24.25 N/2.47 kp DA 47.68 N/4.86 kp
Sight length/line of sight over the barrel axis	192 mm/23 mm
Rear sight width/front sight width	3.3 mm/3.3 mm
Price incl. VAT	725 euros (2011)

*TriggerScan measurements

Trigger Pull Profile [N/mm]

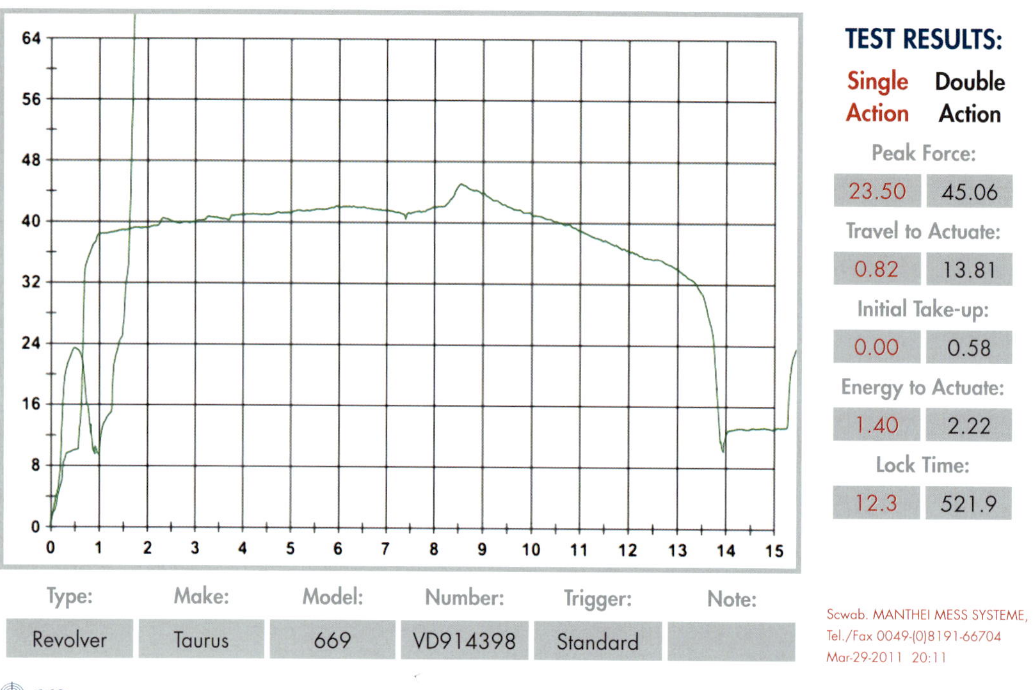

669

Trigger Pull Profile [N/mm]

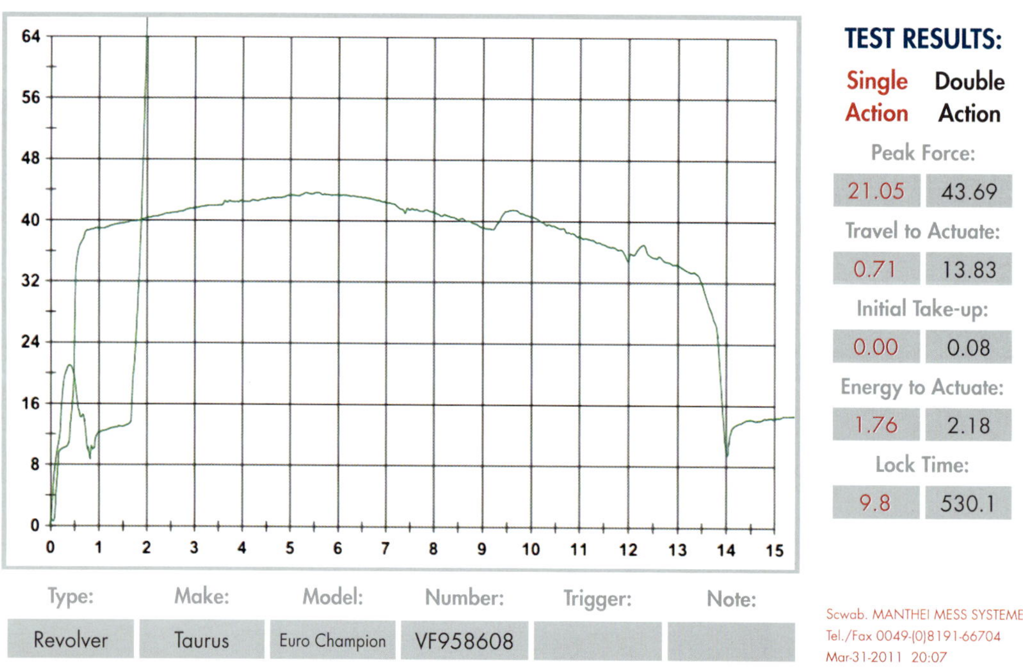

689 Euro Champion

444 Raging Bull

Trigger Pull Profile [N/mm]

617 Ti

Shooting Performance

Revolvers – without requiring either specially long barrels or pricey extras – always shoot well with the right ammunition. Or, as the hunter says: "Most rifles shoot better than the man behind the trigger." Shooting can be even more precise, if the shooter also deals with the reloading press and the ammunition is perfectly suited to the gun.

However, since loading or reloading are not always desired activities, nor done skillfully, there are alternatives, including making a comparison of the revolver's shooting performance when using commercial ammunition from a well-known manufacturer, as it is fired, box after box, on the shooting range.

The following tables show the three best performances each with ten brands in the calibers .38 Special (+ P) and .357 Magnum, four in .44 Special, and six in .44 Magnum. Not all makes and bullet shapes are included in the competition. Negative examples include an otherwise well-placed lead round nose .38, which the Ruger GP100 Frankonia Freestyle 1500 downright rejected, with a group of 66 millimeters, or a lead truncated cone .38, with 72 millimeters from the Taurus 689 Euro Champion. Altogether, the .357 performed somewhat better.

To obtain comparable shooting images at 25 meters, it is essential to have a fixed support and a large enough supply of equal batches of ammunition. Krappmann's replica of a Ransom Rest, completely milled from steel and equipped with a disk brake for high-level impact, filled the first requirement. The second is necessary, not only when the action continues over an extended period, but also for re-shooting, in case of any potential possible problems or widely divergent bullet velocities. Even professionally produced ammunition is not immune to this, as shown by the difference from 274 to 301 meters per second for a Janz JTL .44 Special.

In precision shooting, five out of six hits always count, so that the five-shot Ruger KSP-331X doesn't enjoy the benefit of any stricken results that are not counted. The velocity measurements, registered simultaneously, demonstrate whether the ammunition reached the prescribed minimum impulse in the particular firearm, according to the specifications of the two largest Shooters' Associations – or by how much they surpassed it "without penalty." The *Deutsche Schützenbund* [German Shooting Federation] (DSB) tested for MIPs [*Mindestimpuls*, minimal impulse factors] of 350 and 450 for admission to the two large-caliber Magnum revolver events, based on the formula: 0.1 x bullet weight (g) x muzzle velocity (m/s) (meters/second). The Association of German Sports Shooters [*Bund Deutscher Sportschützen*] (BDS) even requires a five-level gradation for additional potential starters: 100 for revolvers under 4 inches in long-distance shooting; 112.5 for revolvers up to .38; 150 for revolvers over .38 (such as .44 Special and .45 ACP); 180 for .357 Magnum revolvers; and 250 for revolver magnums over .357. Calculations are made based on the formula: bullet weight (g) x 15.432 x muzzle velocity (m/s) x 3.281: 1,000.

Make /Model	Cartridge	Group (mm)*	Vl (m/s)	DSB Factor	BDS Factor
Colt Python /6”	.357 Magnum Geco 10.2 g SJ FP	25”	417	425	215
	.357 Lapua Magnum 9.7 g CEPP	25”	383	372	188
	.357 Magnum Hirtenberger 10.2 g SJ FP	26”	433	442	224
	.38 Special Magtech 10.2 g lead RN	25”	229	—	118
	.38 Special WM Bullets 10.2 g lead FP	27”	247	—	128
	.38 Special Geco 9.6 g WC	28”	188	—	91
Colt Anaconda /6”	.44 Magnum WM Bullets 19.4 g lead TC	30”	314	609	308
	.44 Magnum Winchester 15.6 g SJ FP	32”	314	490	248
	.44 Magnum Magtech 15.6 g SJ FP	35”	366	571	289
	.44 Special Winchester 15.9 g lead RN	32”	233	—	188
	.44 Special WM Bullets 15.6 g lead FP	37”	241	—	190
	.44 Special Magtech 15.6 g lead TC	40”	219	—	173
Smith & Wesson M 686 Distinguished Combat Magnum /6”	.357 Winchester Magnum 10.2 g SJ FP	27	399	407	206
	.357 Lapua Magnum 9.7 g CEPP	28	387	375	190
	.357 Magnum Geco 10.2 g SJ FP	31	371	378	192
	.38 Special Federal 9.6 g WC	28	250	—	129
	.38 Special S & B 10.2 lead RN	29	248	—	128
	.38 Special Magtech 10.2 g lead RN	30	232	—	120

Smith & Wesson M 686 Target Champion /6"	.357 Magnum Fiocchi 10.2 g SJ FP	26	400	408	207
	.357 Winchester Magnum 10.2 g SJ FP	27	404	412	209
	.357 Magnum Hirtenberger 10.2 g SJ FP	29	411	419	212
	.38 Special S&B 10.2 g lead RN	28	293	—	151
	.38 Special IMI 10.2 g SJ FP	31	287	—	148
	.38 Special PMC 10.2 g lead RN	31	299	—	154
Smith & Wesson M 627 Target Champion /6"	.357 Magnum Geco 10.2 g SJ FP	30	358	365	185
	.357 Winchester Magnum 10.2 g SJ FP	30	386	394	199
	.357 Magnum Fiocchi 10.2 g SJ FP	31	368	375	190
	.38 Special S&B 10.2 g lead RN	33	240	—	124
	.38 Special WM Bullets 10.2 g lead FP	34	233	—	120
	.38 Special Magtech 10.2 g lead RN	35	231	—	119
Smith & Wesson M 629 Classic /6 1/2"	.44 Magnum Winchester 15.6 g SJ FP	30	366	571	289
	.44 Magnum Fiocchi 15.6 g SJ FP	33	313	488	247
	.44 Magnum Magtech 15.6 g SJ FP	34	357	557	282
	.44 Special Winchester 15.9 g lead RN	34	228	—	184
	.44 Special WM Bullets 15.6 g lead FP	37	239	—	189
	.44 Special Magtech 15.6 g lead TC	39	217	—	171

Korth Sport Model /6"	.357 Magnum Xapua 9.7 g CEPP	24	380	369	187
	.357 Magnum Hirtenberger 10.2 g SJ FP	25	386	394	199
	.357 Magnum Federal 10.2 g SJ FP	25	398	406	206
	.38 Special S&B 10.2 g lead RN	24	276	—	143
	.38 Special PMC 10.2 g lead RN	26	248	—	128
	.38 Special Magtech 10.2 g lead RN	27	231	—	119
Janz JTX .357 /6"	.357 Magnum Geco 10.2 g SJ FP	24	393	401	203
	.357 Magnum Magtech 10.2 g SJ FP	24	386	394	199
	.357 Magnum Hirtenberger 10.2 g SJ FP	25	408	416	211
	.38 Special Geco 10.2 g FJ RN	24	309	—	160
	.38 Special Geco 9.6 g WC	25	208	—	101
	.38 Special Federal 10.2 g lead RN	29	237	—	122
Janz JTX .44 /6"	.44 Magnum WM Bullets 15.6 g lead FP	29	308	480	243
	.44 Magnum PMC 15.6 g SJ FP	29	418	652	330
	.44 Magnum Magtech 15.6 g SJ FP	31	372	580	294
	.44 Special Winchester 15.9 g lead RN	31	230	—	185
	.44 Special Magtech 15.6 g lead TC	33	217	—	171
	.44 Special WM Bullets 15.6 g lead FP	34	238	—	188

Weihrauch HW 357 Hunter /3"	.357 Magnum Federal 10.2 g SJ FP	28	349	356	180
	.357 Magnum Fiocchi 10.2 g SJ FP	30	335	342	173
	.357 Magnum Hirtenberger 10.2 g SJ FP	32	362	369	187
	.38 Special Geco 10.2 g FJ RN	35	246	—	127
	.38 Special S&B 10.2 g lead RN	35	245	—	127
	.38 Special IMI 10.2 g SJ FP	39	228	—	118
Weihrauch HW 357 Target Trophy Combat /5 3/4"	.357 Magnum IMI 10.2 g FJ RN	26	372	379	192
	.357 Magnum Fiocchi 10.2 g SJ FP	27	371	378	192
	.357 Magnum Federal 10.2 g SJ FP	29	396	404	205
	.38 Special Geco 10.2 g FJ RN	26	284	—	147
	.38 Special WM Bullets 10.2 g lead FP	31	245	—	127
	.38 Special IMI 10.2 g SJ FP	33	239	—	123
Ruger KRH-445 Redhawk 5 1/2"	.44 Magnum WM Bullets 19.4 g lead TC	32	302	586	297
	.44 Magnum Winchester 15.6 g SJ FP	38	310	484	245
	.44 Magnum Magtech 15.6 g SJ FP	39	363	566	287
	.44 Special Winchester 15.9 g lead RN	40	221	—	178
	.44 Special WM Bullets 15.6 g lead FP	46	237	—	187
	.44 Special Magtech 15.6 g lead TC	49	216	—	171

Ruger KSP-331 X /3 1/16"	.357 Magnum Federal 10.2 g SJ FP	38	364	371	188
	.357 Lapua Magnum 9.7 g CEPP	42	354	343	174
	.357 Magnum Geco 10.2 g SJ FP	46	347	354	179
	.38 Special Federal 9.6 g WC	36	215	—	111
	.38 Special WM Bullets 10.2 g lead FP	37	240	—	124
	.38 Special Magtech 10.2 g lead RN	39	220	—	114
Ruger KGP-161 /6"	.357 Magnum Geco 10.2 g SJ FP	28	379	387	196
	.357 Lapua Magnum 9.7 g CEPP	31	390	378	192
	.357 Winchester Magnum 10.2 g SJ FP	36	401	409	207
	.38 Special Geco 9.6 g WC	31	207	—	101
	.38 Special Federal 9.6 g WC	33	237	—	122
	.38 Special Geco 10.2 g FJ RN	34	299	—	154
Ruger GP-100 Frankonia Freestyle 1500 /6"	.357 Magnum IMI 10.2 g FJ RN	28	404	412	209
	.357 Magnum Fiocchi 10.2 g SJ FP	29	388	396	200
	.357 Lapua Magnum 9.7 g CEPP	31	405	393	199
	.38 Special S&B 10.2 g lead RN	29	301	—	155
	.38 Special Federal 9.6 g WC	30	246	—	127
	.38 Special IMI 10.2 g SJ FP	31	286	—	148

Taurus 617 Ti /2"	.357 Winchester Magnum 10.2 g SJ FP	35	312	318	161
	.357 Magnum Fiocchi 10.2 g SJ FP	38	326	333	168
	.357 Lapua Magnum 9.7 g CEPP	38	322	312	158
	.38 Special WM Bullets 10.2 g lead FP	29	223	—	115
	.38 Special Geco 10.2 g FJ RN	34	240	—	124
	.38 Special Geco 9.6 g WC	37	185	—	90
Taurus 669 /6"	.357 Magnum Geco 10.2 g SJ FP	26	394	402	203
	.357 Magnum Magtech 10.2 g SJ FP	26	370	377	191
	.357 WM Bullets 11.3 g lead TC	26	272	307	156
	.38 Special IMI 10.2 g SJ FP	28	275	—	142
	.38 Special Geco 10.2 g FJ RN	30	297	—	153
	.38 Special Geco 9.6 g WC	34	198	—	96
Taurus 689 Euro Champion /6"	.357 Magnum Hirtenberger 10.2 g SJ FP	25	417	425	215
	.357 Magnum S&B 10.2 g SJ FP	25	412	420	213
	.357 Magnum Federal 10.2 g SJ FP	29	430	439	222
	.38 Special WM Bullets 10.2 g lead FP	28	265	—	137
	.38 Special Geco 10.2 g FJ RN	29	310	—	160
	.38 Special Geco 9.6 WC	30	203	—	99

* Resp. on shot hole centers